Doug Van
Valkenburgh
4 27 74

ABOUT PATERSON

ABOUT

NEW YORK

PATERSON

THE MAKING AND UNMAKING OF AN AMERICAN CITY

Christopher Norwood

SATURDAY REVIEW PRESS | E. P. DUTTON & CO., INC.

Library of Congress Cataloging in Publication Data

Norwood, Christopher.
About Paterson.

1. Paterson, N.J.—Politics and government.
2. Paterson, N.J.—Social conditions. I. Title.
F144.P4N67   320.9'749'2404   73-17112

First Edition

10 9 8 7 6 5 4 3 2 1

Published simultaneously in Canada by Clarke, Irwin & Company,
Limited, Toronto and Vancouver
ISBN: 0-8415-0308-7
Designed by the Etheredges

ACKNOWLEDGMENTS

The news reporters of the city of Paterson, including members of the *Morning Call,* the *Paterson News,* and the *Passaic Herald,* have been of invaluable help to me and their kindnesses are too many to enumerate. However, since the *Morning Call* has now been sold, I would especially like to say that its entire staff was one of rare quality and especially to thank in particular Johnny Chick, for his insights into the Paterson Police Department and Edward Norton, without whose coverage of the labyrinth that is New Jersey politics it would simply not have been possible to write this book. I would also like to express appreciation for the services of the Paterson Public Library, the New York Historical Society, and the Passaic County Historical Society; without Mr. Edward Gaff's years of devotion to the underbudgeted facilities at Lambert's Castle, much of Paterson's history, no doubt, would have been lost. I also appreciate Professor Paul Ylvisaker's taking the time to read the manuscript and greatly appreciate the extensive efforts of my editor Nancy Uberman and editorial assistant Susan Schaeffer. And, finally, I would like to acknowledge a debt to the late William Carlos Williams for those many things that are better said through poetry than through facts.

ABOUT PATERSON

> *An incredible*
> *clumsiness of address*
> *senseless rapes—caught on hands and knees*
> *scrubbing a greasy corridor; the blood*
> *boiling as though in a vat, where they soak—*
>
> *Plaster saints, glass jewels*
> *and those apt paper flowers, bafflingly*
> *complex—have here*
> *their forthright beauty, beside . . .*

—WILLIAM CARLOS WILLIAMS
Paterson *

Every fifteen minutes Inter-City Transportation Company's Number 30 bus leaves the Port Authority Terminal in New York City. After passing under the Hudson River, via the Lincoln Tunnel, the Number 30 passes through a few miles of industrialized wasteland, noted chiefly for its odor. It then veers off Route 3, continuing along tree-bordered suburban roads. Some sixteen miles later the bus arrives at its destination—Paterson, New Jersey. The city lies, sliced in half by the Passaic River, like a piece of old toast.

No sign marks the border between Clifton, a thriving

suburban neighbor, and Paterson, a city conceived by Alexander Hamilton to become the industrial showplace of a young nation. Instead, there is only an air of staleness as one approaches the heart of the city. The crumbs of civilization appear—garbage and broken glass on the sidewalks, the burned-out shell of a tenement, groups of people lounging at corners or staring from the stoops of their homes. A visitor may have difficulty believing he is still in the same country that has produced the nearby Empire State Building as a national symbol of grandeur. The skyscraper is easily visible from the surrounding hills, but along Main Street in Paterson there are neither skyscrapers nor any buildings over five stories. Most of the structures are wooden tenements, their paint long lost. They look as much like the unfinished products of an underdeveloped nation as what they are—the victims of a century of neglect.

About 24 million Americans now live in cities such as Paterson, with populations ranging from 100,000 to one-half million inhabitants. These urban areas are too small to command as much attention as a major city, but they are large enough to develop the same problems. In Paterson the facts are as follows: Some 150,000 citizens occupy 8.36 square miles, making it the fourth most densely populated city in the United States. One out of eight persons is on welfare. At an altitude of eighty feet above sea level, the city has the worst air pollution of any American city its size. Of 219 miles of streets, 214 are paved. About fifteen percent of the population is foreign-born. The base economy is industrial, with some businesses still manufacturing textiles and related goods, which were once the city's major products. The chief growth industries are now electric and small metal products, rubber, plastics, and instruments. The city has twenty-five public and thirteen parochial schools and two daily newspapers.

For its size, Paterson has contributed an unusual assortment of famous sons to the nation. "Leaping" Sam Patch, a cotton-mill foreman, became the only man to jump the Niagara Falls successfully without a protective device. Garrett Augustus Hobart, a city lawyer, became the twenty-fourth vice-president of the United States. Sam Colt produced his first revolver in Paterson, and John Holland tested the first practical submarine on the Passaic River. But most revealing of Paterson's character, the city has been home to two major American poets and two assassins.

While there is no Bureau of Vital Statistics on Poets and Assassins in Washington, it seems safe to say that Paterson is the only American city with this distinction. Nor is it an accident. For Paterson is a prototypical American city, reflecting the fierce strains of hope and despair, of triumph and defeat, of myth and reality that are the enigmas of the American dream. In 1946 William Carlos Williams, a doctor who had been drawn to the city as a distillation of American life, published the first canto of his six-book poem *Paterson*. The "forthright beauty" he evoked from rancid streets and rancid souls inspired a literary explosion against machines and materialism. But it was only fitting that a poem about Paterson—itself the first city in the United States expressly founded for industry—should confront the wastelands of industrialism. Allen Ginsberg grew up in the city, listening to the grating machinery, breathing the polluted atmosphere, and came to express Paterson's long and quixotic search for human values in the midst of the brutal materialism which has ruled it. The city's turbulent atmosphere also produced Angelo Bresci, an anarchist who murdered King Humbert I at the turn of the century, and Talmadge Hayer, who led two other men in the shooting of Black Muslim leader Malcolm X.

In addition to its famous sons, Paterson has recorded a

priceless lesson in American urbanization. Unlike New York, Paterson does not gloss over its truths with museums, theaters, and gleaming skyscrapers. Paterson is not a world capital; it is just another American city. From the time Paterson's first cotton mill went up until its most recent riot, history has been relentless for the city. Its scars are as sharp as the spire on top of the Empire State Building in the distance. Even, its Main Street is devoid of the usual facade of well-kept shops and commercial cleanliness. There is no need to search out back alleys to discover Paterson. By simply getting off the bus on Main Street where it enters South Paterson and walking down to City Hall, a stranger can learn much about this city, which is a living metaphor of the American urban crisis.

The time is early autumn 1968, a time which brought Paterson and many other American cities to a crossroads. The city finds itself caught between reform and machine government. It has been stunned by a riot and is as uncertain of its prospects as it is undecided about the methods and measures it should adopt to face the future.

South Paterson still maintains its character as a working-class area. Most of the homes are two-family houses, old but not yet divided into the ever smaller apartments holding ever larger numbers of people that make a ghetto. Further along the street, literally on the other side of the railroad tracks, the changing conditions overtaking the whole city can be seen. Most striking are the number of Spanish stores and bodegas and the language heard spoken on the street. As elsewhere in Paterson, the southern section contains pockets of the Old World where Italians, Russians, Jews, and even a smattering of Gypsies still speak their own languages and retain their own customs. In the 1940s Allen Ginsberg expressed his excitement at discovering these places in his "struggle to love and know his own world city." Ginsberg particularly remarked on the Gypsies, who still remain a source of apprehensive fascination to the neighborhood. When a tenement recently burned down on Main Street, the fire department reported without qualification that twenty-one families and one band of Gypsies had been left homeless. "Those people—you know —the Gypsies," the fire lieutenant explained gingerly, not quite certain if "Gypsy," like "colored," had joined the ranks of words no longer used.

The new population is mostly Spanish and, until recently, the older immigrants got along fairly well with their Puerto Rican neighbors, perhaps thinking it was better to have them than the blacks. This feeling was interrupted in July by a riot, which the city administration quickly dubbed a "disturbance." Occasionally, when trying to explain urban turmoil to suburban audiences, the incumbent mayor, Lawrence F. Kramer, has also termed the riot "a bad Goosey Night." * Whatever its description, the riot did not create deep enmity toward the Puerto Ricans mainly because general opinion decided to blame it on the blacks. The riot was considered to be a fluke, "out of character" for the Puerto Ricans and, therefore, the work of "outside agitators"—meaning militants from the central Fourth Ward ghetto. In reality, the riot was neither "in" nor "out of" character for the Puerto Ricans; it was simply the turn of the Spanish. Paterson's history has been characterized by the continuing process of immigrant adjustment, which has seen almost every successive

* Goosey Night is the night before Halloween, an event that is vigorously celebrated in Paterson by children and teenagers roaming the streets and causing trouble. The author has been unable to trace the origins of this custom, but it seems likely that it developed from ancient religious practices, probably imported by some immigrant groups, of preparing for All Saints' Day by going out into the darkness and making noise to frighten away ghosts and evil spirits. The name "Goosey Night" may be a reference to the "goose flesh" that this fearful confrontation with the spirits gave rise to.

group, including the Germans, Italians, and Negroes, take its rage to the streets at some point.

The next important sight on Main Street is the Lawrence F. Kramer Company, a small building in back of which are piled the bricks and construction materials that constitute the trade of the incumbent mayor. The company does little business these days and is usually closed. The mayor has too many tribulations to pay attention to it. A young Republican long-shot who won on a reform platform in 1966 in a city with a 7–to–1 Democratic registration, Kramer has not found governing Paterson to be so gratifying as he had expected. Nearly next door to the Lawrence F. Kramer Company is St. Joseph's, the city's largest hospital, founded a century ago by the Sisters of Charity. Sister Anne Jean, the administrator, has announced "most reluctantly" that St. Joseph's financial condition now necessitates turning away indigent patients for the first time in its history. Mayor Kramer's opponents have seized on this announcement as yet another shocking proof of his failure to provide for the city's needs.

A block past St. Joseph's is the "G" Industrial Corporation and Public Relations firm. By 1968 the firm was handling the public relations of only one person, its proprietor, who wants to be mayor for a third term. Former Mayor Frank X. Graves, after serving his city for two three-year terms from 1961 through 1966, was barred by law from succeeding himself again. Acting as the head of a government in exile, Graves has spent the last two years waiting and preparing to reclaim the office which he regards as his almost by right.

Inside the "G" Industrial Corporation, which is nothing more than a downstairs office and second-floor conference room with a kitchenette, Frank X. Graves practices politics as the art of a thousand backroom lessons inspired by the brazenness of success. He is of average height. His hair has started disappearing. When he is relaxed, his blue eyes take on an arresting transluscence which makes one note, almost unexpectedly, that Frank Graves is a handsome man. But ordinarily one doesn't notice his individual features, for he is one of those unusual men whose total presence is over-whelming—almost like an assault. Today he is electric, absorbed in building his strength for the election of 1969, more than a year away. "I always do my homework," he explains.

The phone rings continually; supplicants come to the door. Graves has two complimentary passes to the race track, which are cheerfully placed in different hands every day. A young woman arrives to pick them up and jokes with Graves for a minute. She is followed by an elderly fireman, holding his hat carefully in front of him, who feels he has been unfairly passed over for promotion. Graves will look into it. The Reverend James Jackson, head of the Afro-American Cadets, reminds the former mayor about the group's fund-raising dinner, and Graves takes an ad in the dinner program. A Puerto Rican woman returns his call. "Look, I'm telling you. I need your help to get back into office," Graves informs her. "If I do, I'll be fair to your people. Didn't I put the first Puerto Rican on the police force?" He did not add, the first of only two.

The last two years have been about the worst of Graves' life. He has been a force in the city for almost all his adult years, serving first as a city alderman, then county commissioner and, finally, as mayor. When in office, Graves was known as "the twenty-four-hour mayor," not because he slept at City Hall, but because he used the powers of his office to direct the city's movements night and day. A man who must be active, Graves enjoyed being mayor for the pulse alone. "It's the only job that changes every day. You might have your desk cleared by 9:15 and all of a sudden the whole place breaks loose." Even now, when he parks his Oldsmobile 88, he leaves all the equipment—including the air conditioner, standard radio, and the police radio that lets him monitor the city's breathing—turned on, ready for action. Previously he often answered the police calls himself. Now he can't do that and sometimes he becomes so bored that he drives to New York, with all his equipment on instant alert, and goes to the movies by himself.

Even out of office, Graves is considered the most powerful man in the city; but this is no consolation for the precise gratifications of command that were his life force. Yet his feelings for the office involve more than personal ambition. Graves considers himself the single politician in Paterson who is not only capable of running the city, but who also understands the methods required to get the job done. Being mayor, therefore, is both his duty and his prerogative. He made it his business to know the city better than anyone—its idiosyncracies, its moods, its fears. He turned this knowledge not just to governing Paterson, but to ruling it and bullying it when he thought that approach was appropriate.

To assure that the city would function during the three years of his enforced retirement, Graves assigned a lieutenant to occupy the mayor's seat for him. However, the 1966 election went awry and Kramer won. The fact that Paterson voted for Kramer does not interest Graves. If the city erred and chose a man who is "destroying" it, Graves' task is clear; he must stop that man. Graves utterly disdains "the Boy Scout," as he calls Kramer. All visitors to the "G" Industrial Corporation are treated to a nonstop harangue on the latest sins of the incumbent. Kramer, according to Graves, has no idea how to govern Paterson. He is permitting the city to run wild. He has demoralized the police department and assured a rise in crime. His liberalism and lack of force encourage a riotous atmosphere. His "big spending programs" are breaking the taxpayers.

The struggle between the new mayor and the old mayor

is, however, more than a matter of either policy or politics. It is a dispute that centers on a fundamental conception of the city. In Graves' opinion, Paterson can only survive with "a strong mayor," a man who will set himself over the city, make it obey, and never permit it to stumble on its own passions and divisions—or waste its energy pursuing its own opinions. The mayor, in short, is the city. All responsibility and all decisions rest on his shoulders. Critics, opponents, community groups with their proposals, and the newspapers with their editorials do not really count. They did not, by drive, energy, or cunning, win their way to the mayor's office and obtain the incontrovertible right to speak for the city. For Graves, the Paterson mayoralty constitutes the ultimate elective office. He would have disliked Kramer for taking it away under any circumstances. That Kramer also refuted Graves' concept of Paterson was like a refutation of the former mayor's existence. But, in an odd way, Graves would have disdained his rival less if Kramer had been completely successful. The young man's apparent political impotence in handling the title and rights that Graves handled so lustily are an insult to the office of the mayor and an insult to the city.

Graves' term in office was a relentless example of his personal theory for governing Paterson. Despite the contempt for the democratic process that this sometimes entailed, he made a strong impression on many people that his view, ultimately, is the right one. His craft and energy in moving Paterson, his ability to knock down obstacles were unexcelled. He answered to no one because he never doubted that he knew all the answers himself. He imposed his brash egoism on the city's weaknesses and molded them into a precise instrument of command. This extraordinary skill could have made him the best mayor in Paterson's history—and perhaps the best mayor in the United States. His administration was marred, however, by one grand jury presentment on Board of Education purchasing practices, another grand jury investigation of school construction, a grand jury probe of alleged police brutality, and one of the first urban riots to presage the rioting wave of the 1960s.

Next door to the "G" Industrial Corporation is WXTV, a Spanish-language UHF television station that occupies two one-story windowless concrete buildings. Mr. Graves is fond of calling it "my TV station." He is only the landlord of the buildings, but his language creates the fear in other politicians, as it is meant to, that he has a powerful means to influence the city's Spanish-speaking population, which is heading toward fifteen percent.

Some two blocks farther along the broken sidewalk lies a vacant lot that particularly rankles the city. A sign from the New Jersey Department of Transportation declares "Highway Taxes at Work." No work has been done since 1964. The sign has been there for four years, marking the course of Interstate Route 80, an eight-lane superhighway destined to stretch from New York to California. Paterson's residents place great hopes on the completion of the road, believing its easy access to New York will revitalize local industry, lure shoppers to the downtown business section, and generally perform the thousand miracles that haven't come from any other source. Like Paterson itself, the superhighway is the victim of the city's own self-strangulating politics, an indifferent state government, and a federal government which has failed domestic needs. The routing was long delayed by bitter local quarrels over the road's alignment, and subsequent spoils from property sales. The state commissioner of transportation was formerly the governor's personal attorney. "I just don't think he knows much about building roads," says one local official. The road was further delayed when the federal government, because of the needs of the Vietnam war, cut off funding.

Route 80, when finally completed, would span eleven states from New York's George Washington Bridge to the Golden Gate Bridge in San Francisco. In 1968 the 2,900 miles were seventy-five percent complete. New Jersey, which had only to build sixty-eight miles, the least of any state, in ten years had finished twenty-five miles, again the least of any state. The last section in Paterson was then estimated for completion in 1975 and the planners conceded it might well turn out to be the last section of the entire 2,900 miles, making it possible to drive across the breadth of the United States —through Pennsylvania, Illinois, Iowa, Indiana, Ohio, Nebraska, Wyoming, Utah, Nevada, and California—but not Paterson, New Jersey. One of Mayor Kramer's most effective devices in his 1966 election campaign was a poster of him standing, superimposed over Route 80's abrupt end. "The road goes on from here," said the caption. It attracted the city's imagination. But the road has not yet progressed one inch. Instead, Pat Kramer, as he is nicknamed, is about that close to losing his post.

Across Main Street, Garrett Mountain, which is actually a large hill, rises about the city. Near the top Lambert's Castle, built in 1894 by the city's largest silk manufacturer, mocks the dreary scene below and recalls past glories when Paterson was known as "The Silk City of the United States." Now owned by the Passaic County Historical Society, the castle is a hulking medieval structure, whose turretted stone battlements have been modified for the convenience of installing large glass double windows. When a visitor first notices it looming above the woods of the Garrett Mountain reservation it is an overwhelming sight. Unlike the mayor, Mr. Lambert had no road or transportation problems; he hired special trains to bring 400 guests to the castle's opening reception. The city still holds an annual May Day celebration on the mountain, a custom started by German immigrants.

The contrast between two luncheonettes, just blocks apart, illustrates the changes spreading toward the city's edges. The Colonial Tea Room, run by Ethel, a woman of about forty-five who keeps her hair ensconced in a net, is directly across from St. Joseph's. The waitresses at the Tea Room wear white uniforms, and everything is crisp and neat, including the clientele, mainly employees from the hospital. Ethel minds her own business and rarely talks about herself, even with customers she has been seeing daily for years. Nonetheless, she has strong opinions on public affairs. In the upcoming mayoralty race she is "Rootin' for Rooney," as the slogan goes. Thomas Rooney, a conservative and the president of the Taxpayers Association, is running for the second time as an independent. "If you ask me, the last time, the only thing Graves left behind was City Hall," she says. "People in Paterson must be out of their minds to want to go through that again. I say give Rooney a chance. All those politicians have already had their turn and look at the mess they made." Ethel also has a dream. "All I ask is to be out of this country in ten years when these revolutionary kids have taken over."

Several doors down from WXTV is a luncheonette officially named Ramon's, but always called Ramona's after the wife of the proprietor. Ramona, a native of Puerto Rico, is a local personage who keeps close track of happenings in the neighborhood. Both she and her quiet, soft-spoken husband, Willy, are unpretentiously generous. Ramona instinctively recognizes when any child, white, black, or Puerto Rican, hasn't eaten recently. She pushes a hamburger in front of the kid with her customary invitation, "Take it." An endless number of relatives and in-laws man the counter haphazardly. In the mornings the stranded people—the retired people who can't afford to move out, men without work, and a few unbalanced souls—sit around for hours over the same ten-cent cup of coffee. Ramona's was one of the few stores in the area with its windows intact after the riot. Ramona is supporting Kramer in the election. "I know him long time," she says of Graves, "and I see. All the time he has the police, the police. This is no good for the people." Willy feels Kramer is willing to do things for the Spanish. "But you have to ask nice, ask the right way," he observes.

In another few blocks is the crossroads of Paterson, where Main Street meets Market Street, a corner formed by one bank and three jewelry stores. Here the life of the city continually passes by: shoppers, gangs of kids, squad cars from the nearby police headquarters, family groups, often speaking Spanish, Italian, or Yiddish among themselves. Twice a month there is an incredible traffic jam at the corner as welfare recipients crowd the New Jersey Bank to cash their checks. Although it is a lively crossroads, there is also an apprehensive feeling in the air. Just as Paterson's residents are unsure where their city as a whole is going, so they can never be sure when its center will turn on them. Kids dart into the street and stop traffic for no reason. Arguments and incidents arise without warning. The elderly bums who spend their day sunning and drinking on the benches in front of City Hall sometimes drop dead in the middle of the sidewalk while walking home.

The city's underlying rawness can emerge suddenly, even in the midst of banks and department stores. Two black children, about three and seven years old, wander the street by themselves. They enter the open door of a camera shop. A Kodak display—a cardboard stand-up woman wearing a bikini and holding out a box of film with a tempting smile—attracts the elder. He throws his arms around the blonde paper woman and pretends to kiss and fondle her. The customers and the manager of the store watch in speechless horror. The child clearly knows what he is doing. The toddler, delighted by the game, runs up to the Kodak lady and mimics his brother. The older child slaps him. "Hey, you," he says. "Get offa that white woman. You know you ain't allowed to get on that white woman." Finally the manager collects himself enough to emit a strangled directive. "Get out," he stammers. The boys run out and nobody says a word. What can they say? They know without comment that, along with color prints of birthday parties and bar mitzvahs, a seven-year-old who understands "getting on" a woman is part of a day in Paterson.

Within view, a block down Market Street, is City Hall and the men who run this 8.36 square miles. Mayor Lawrence F. Kramer occupies a spacious room on the second floor of the imposing ornate building that was designed by Carrere and Hastings at the turn of the century and is crowned with a clock tower. Kramer is thirty-five years old, has brown hair and blue eyes, and is good-looking in the slightly rugged, compact way that indicates he played football in high school. He is the democratically elected municipal chief of all he surveys—of Ethel and Ramona and Frank X. Graves and a child assaulting a cardboard woman. He can regularly look down to the street and watch Metzler's Ambulance Service remove the most recently expired bum. Twice a month the honking from the welfare jam becomes so annoying that he calls the police department with the same message. "Jesus, can't you get a traffic man on that corner?"

The mayor's office is neatly and sparsely furnished. An oil painting of his wife and two oldest children dominates the room. On the wall to the left of his desk is a framed quotation from Lincoln: "If the end brings me out all right, what is said against me won't amount to anything. If the end brings me out wrong, ten angels swearing I was right would make no difference." On the right is a small bookcase filled with historical volumes and topped off by a bit of Paterson memorabilia—one of the gold spikes pounded into the last link of the first complete rail line between East and West. (The spike was recently returned to Paterson in honor of the city's contribution to the development of American railroads.)

Kramer is outgoing and friendly; on the surface he appears to be enthusiastic about his work. Whatever subject he is discussing, he likes to dwell on what he calls "bold, exciting new concepts." A playground under Route 80 is an example of the bold concept of using unoccupied space to make children happy. A middle-income housing project being sponsored by the United Automobile Workers' Union is exciting because it will attract people to live in the downtown area. Only an excessive smoothness, a reliance on public-relations jargon, reveals that Kramer's enthusiasm is rehearsed. Recent setbacks have taken a toll on the mayor, but even so he would still appear to have good reason to be satisfied. His position is rewarding and challenging; it is also promising. New Jersey has a dearth of what the local papers call "bright, young Republicans" and Kramer is already being mentioned as a long shot for governor. New York Mayor John V. Lindsay, when he was still encouraging "the liberal, reform wing" of the Republican party, sent advisors to help Kramer with his 1966 campaign. With Nixon about to enter the White House and being one of the few big-city Republican mayors, Kramer is finding himself the object of flattering attention from Washington. His wife, Mary Ellen, whom he met at a Catholic Youth Organization dance in Paterson, and his three children love him.

But the notice of a president, a good chance of becoming

a governor or senator, a handsome and close-knit family—
none of them is quite enough. The blue eyes, which everyone
knows captured the votes of many women, have a haunted
edge. Neither the outward indices of Kramer's success nor
the promise of a bright future can cover the failures of the
present—or change the fact that he is sitting in his office beneath a quote from Lincoln, mouthing words that he thinks
he is required to say, but which he no longer firmly believes.
There was a time when he didn't speak to Paterson in public-
relations phrases. He spoke loudly and clearly about corruption, slums, human rights, and decency. Paterson responded
and voted him into its highest office. But change in Paterson
was not that simple, because no matter what the city wants
or what he, its elected leader, wants, neither is in a position
to get it. A hundred other forces—the federal government,
the state legislature, the political machines, the banks, the
real-estate interests, the construction industry, the Mafia, the
county prosecutor—rule Paterson.

And so, with Graves trying to regain his grip on the past
and Kramer searching for his foothold on the future, the two
opponents look out over Paterson from opposite ends of Main
Street, each in his own way as frustrated as the city itself.
Neither is certain who is winning. For all his assertions that
he is right and that he knows Paterson, Graves lives with an
uneasy feeling that the city has changed in some subtle, essential way from the one he controlled. As stung as Kramer has
been by his mistakes and defeats, the memory of that magic
day two years ago when Paterson arose and said yes taunts
him with the possibility that Paterson may really become his.
It is only one of Paterson's many ironies that Lawrence F.
Kramer and Frank X. Graves should be locked in a death
struggle for whatever life Paterson has. They grew up on the
same street, their businesses are a few blocks apart, they both
attend St. Theresa's Roman Catholic Church, and each in his

turn became the youngest mayor in city history. Yet to the city they symbolize a choice that has so bitterly divided it as to put family and friends on nonspeaking terms and cause businessmen to dissolve partnerships.

In appealing to their constituencies, both Graves and Kramer deliberately played upon this symbolism by assuming caricatures of their political roles. Depending on which side was speaking, the city's choice was simple; it was between liberal and conservative, individual integrity against the machine, justice versus law and order. However, these slogans did not define the true question facing Paterson; and its choice, like that of other cities, was not so straightforward as a decision between the policies of two candidates for the mayor's office. The question facing Paterson was whether or not it could become a place that realized the promise of American democracy, a city where its citizens were genuinely respected and represented. Paterson had already spent nearly two centuries trying to answer this question and the struggle between Graves and Kramer merely brought it into immediate focus. The city's fight was not between political candidates, but a fight against a country that has traditionally used its cities as the worst expression of itself.

This, then, is Paterson, New Jersey. It began as an urban experiment meant to stand as a monument to American might and prestige. Like other American cities, it has been destroyed—if not intentionally, then clearly not by accident. The tour of Main Street, with its pitiless mementos of the city's downfall, is over. A stranger should not be blamed if it has taken him a conscious act of courage to walk down the street. Its mundane name, Main Street, with its visions of such familiar scenes as drugstore soda fountains and white porches, clashes violently with the street's actual appearance.

Main Street does hold a menace which, at first, seems to be the usual threat of a developing slum—the intimidating groups of corner loiterers, buildings that look as though they would be pleased to collapse at a passerby's feet, and the general feeling that time itself has fled and cares no more. But sometime later, if the visitor came to know and love the city, he would also know that Main Street is paved in the torment of all roads that stretch between an unusable past and a future unfounded.

*If the material power and splendor of the state be
the great end of statesmanship, no just complaint
can be lodged against such a policy; but if the well-
being of the individual citizen be the chief end, a
very different judgment must be returned.*

—UNIDENTIFIED
(*Possibly Alexander Hamilton*)

Paterson may well be the most instructive city in the United
States for exploring the roots of the American urban crisis.
It was, of course, not meant to become a city whose main
thoroughfare is edged by tenements and the scene of bi-
monthly welfare traffic jams. It was designed to become,
among other things, the largest and most elegant city in the
United States, a "national manufactory," and a majestic symbol of American power. It was the first American city to be
specifically founded as an industrial center. More important,
the city's founding in 1792 represented a radical turning
point in the direction of the young republic. In the singular
vision of industrial might, empire, and corporate power that

inspired the city's beginnings, it might be said that the future of the United States, and, more specifically, the future of American cities, was essentially decided.

In July 1778, Colonel Alexander Hamilton, General George Washington, the Marquis de Lafayette, and his aide-de-camp, Colonel James McHenry, were heading for the war camp at Paramus, New Jersey. Riding through the wooded hills, home of the Lenni Lenape Indians and a few Dutch farmers, they paused to enjoy a scenic lunch by the Passaic Falls as has been recorded in McHenry's diary:

> The travelling canteens were immediately emptied and a modest repast spread before us, of cold ham, tongue and some biscuits, with the assistance of a little spirits, we composed some excellent grog, then chatted away a very cheerful half hour—then took our leave of the friendly oak—its refreshing spring—and the meek falls of the Passaic.*

The small town nestled below the falls consisted of ten houses and the Godwin Tavern. A main street called "Peace and Plenty Lane" reflected the character of this simple farming community. It is hard to imagine that here in this quiet setting would culminate an intense struggle of power and philosophy among the Founding Fathers. It was a contest between industry and agriculture, between centralized government and "the power of the people," between the "splendor of the state" and the "well-being of the individual citizen." Fourteen years later Hamilton chose the site of his hasty picnic for an experiment meant to change the destiny of the United States.

Alexander Hamilton was the most vigorous of the

* Bernard Steiner, *The Life and Correspondence of James McHenry* (Cleveland: Burrows Brothers, 1907), p. 22.

Founding Fathers in advocating a strong national government. Building federal strength and wealth was his burning preoccupation, the end toward which he would use any means. He regarded power as the supreme mission of the new government for a simple reason; like most people at the time, he had grave doubts that the government could last. The federal authority, he felt, did not have time to wait for the consensus and support of its citizens; it had to insure its own survival by developing the strongest resources as quickly as possible. Hamilton did not hold the "romantic" opinion that the nation's resources lay in flourishing farms, a modestly contented people, and "mild" government. For him resources meant factories and commerce; and above all he believed that the federal government could best build its own strength by aligning itself with the industrial complex.*

As a leader of the Federalists and first Secretary of the Treasury, Hamilton moved to undercut the agrarian economic bias of his day and proposed instead to centralize the economy through industrialization. He saw this move as the only way America could guarantee its freedom both domestically and internationally. A strong economic policy would insure domestic liberty and guard America's freedom of movement in the world. A rich, productive country, he maintained, could never become "despicable by its weakness" in its dealings with other nations; and a government with strong resources at its command need not fear overthrow and anarchy at home.†

Among the difficulties of molding thirteen colonies into one nation, it was domestic anarchy that haunted Hamilton

---

* "Report on Manufacturers," *The Papers of Alexander Hamilton*, Harold C. Spratt and Jacob E. Cooke, eds., Vol. X (New York: The Columbia University Press, 1961), p. 340.

† "A nation, despicable by its weakness, forfeits even the privilege of being neutral." The Federalist #11, *Papers of Hamilton*, Vol. IV, p. 32.

above all else.* Although he often disparaged "the people,"
Hamilton did not believe that any future threat to the federal authority would come as a result of action taken by the
masses; it was the powerful whom he profoundly mistrusted.†
Any government that wished to survive, he thought, would
take the practical precaution of handling its most powerful
citizens with care. If men with resources and wealth grew
dissatisfied, they would certainly be more dangerous than a
few farmers staging a "whiskey rebellion." The government's
duty, therefore, was to protect the people from this threat.
If Hamilton did not actually call the people "a great beast,"
as has been said, he did consider them too weak to protect
themselves.

Moreover, the Jeffersonian belief that the "American
experience" would produce leaders of unequaled morality
and benevolence struck Hamilton as an absurd and deadly
illusion.‡ He believed that the only way the government
could fulfill its duty of guarding the country from tyranny
was by winning the cooperation of its most powerful citizens.
It followed that the only way of satisfying the powerful was
to make the government's policies vital to their well-being.
"By means of this [self] interest, we must govern [them], and
by means of it make [them] cooperate to the public good, notwithstanding [their] insatiable avarice and ambition," Hamilton wrote. "Without this, we shall in vain boast of the
advantages of any Constitution, and shall find in the end, that
we have no security for our liberty and possessions, except

---

* Hamilton used the strongest terms to describe his hatred of anarchy, writ-
ing, for example, in The Federalist #91 that it was impossible to read the
checkered history of "the petty Republics of Greece and Italy, without feeling
sensations of horror and disgust" at their extremes of tyranny and anarchy.
Papers of Hamilton, Vol. IV, p. 333.
† The Continentalist #1, *Papers of Hamilton,* Vol. II, p. 652.
‡ See also Clinton Rossiter, *Alexander Hamilton and the Constitution* (New
York: Harcourt Brace and World, 1964).

the good will of our rulers; that is, we shall have no security at all." *

There were those among Hamilton's critics who felt he surmounted this obstacle quite simply by making avarice and "the public good" synonymous. Today there may be anger over individual acts of corruption in the federal favoring of corporations; but the concept that the business of the American government is business is rarely questioned. In the 1790s Hamiltonian encroachments on what was supposed to have been a rural democracy nearly brought down the government. The opposition was so intense that most historians feel only George Washington's immense prestige as president kept the country from dissolving.

If Hamilton considered industry essential, the Republicans, led by Thomas Jefferson, considered an agrarian economy as the necessary, almost sacred base of the nation they envisioned.† They felt that democratic principles could not survive in an industrial society. In their view government centralization, at first financial, would end by repression in all quarters. As the legislature of Virginia protested in a resolution to Congress, the government backing of capitalist entrepreneurs must "produce one or the other of two evils: the prostration of agriculture at the feet of commerce or a change in the present form of the Federal Government fatal to the existence of American liberty." A government alliance with industry would give rise to a new aristocracy with the concentrated wealth and power to strangle individual independence. "Which is most to be dreaded; titles without wealth, or exorbitant wealth without titles?" demanded one critic. "Money in a state of civilization is power." ‡

Sub-servience [margin note]

* The Farmer Refuted, *Papers of Hamilton*, Vol. I, p. 95.
† Charles A. Beard, *Economic Origins of Jeffersonian Democracy.* (New York: The Macmillan Company, 1915; Free Press Paperback ed., 1965), pp. 421–22.
‡ John Taylor, *Inquiry into the Principles and Tendencies of Certain Public Measures,* 1794.

The Jeffersonians did not base their dislike of industry solely on philosophical grounds; they dreaded its practical effects on the nation. Jefferson viewed cities with their discontented masses as chief among the corruptions of Europe. Industry robbed people of the dignity of controlling their own lives. "Cultivators of the earth are the most valuable citizens, the most independent, the most virtuous," Jefferson declared, "and they are tied to their country, and wedded to its liberty and interests, by the most lasting bonds. . . . I consider the class of artificers [mechanics and craftsmen] as the panders of vice and the instruments by which the liberties of a country are generally overturned." * Jefferson, in fact, considered industrial concentration so dangerous to democracy that it would be well worth the extra expense to keep importing manufactured goods from Europe. "The loss by the transportation of commodities across the Atlantic," he felt, "will be made up by the happiness and permanence of government. The mobs of great cities add just so much to the support of pure government, as sores do to the strength of the human body. It is the manners and spirit of a people which preserve a republic in vigor. A degeneracy in these is a canker which soon eats to the heart of its laws and constitution." †

Jefferson, no doubt, represented prevailing public sentiment. Hamilton represented something more powerful—the future. As stringently as Jefferson denounced "the corrupt squadron" in the Treasury Department, Hamilton, using the time-honored political tools of gerrymandering, lobbying, a fine appreciation for the means which induce congressmen to "cooperate to the public good," prevailed in laying the foundations for his vision. His measures—funding the

---

* John C. Riker, *The Works of Thomas Jefferson*, Vol. I, Washington ed. (New York, 1857), p. 403.
† Notes on Virginia, Riker, *The Works of Thomas Jefferson*, Vol. XIII, p. 406.

national debt, establishing the Bank of the United States, instituting paper currency and taxes—centralized the economy and provided the basis for commercial and industrial expansion. His proposal for Paterson was the only important aspect of his plans he failed to get through Congress. He wanted the government to allocate $1 million (then two percent of the national debt) to build a "national manufactory." He envisioned the proposed city as a huge, model industrial complex where the country would concentrate its capital and skills and acquire the industrial supremacy to guarantee America a strong, independent role in world affairs.

This was perhaps the most extraordinary urban proposal ever made in America by a person with both the ability and the potential power to carry out his plans. Had Hamilton succeeded, the barely established government would have entered the business of founding and planning cities. The government would have also become the nation's chief manufacturer—a strangely socialist concept from the man who is regarded as the archconservative of the Founding Fathers. However, Hamilton realized that the Congress, already hostile to many of his policies, would not accept another increase in federal power. Instead, he sought private backers to begin his experiment.

Although the federal government did not, therefore, directly found Paterson, the policies of the Jeffersonians and Federalists irrevocably stamped it and other American cities. For Hamilton, cities were not vital centers—a "second body to the human mind," as Santayana put it—they were simply conveniences, a means toward industrialization. Jefferson's outlook, on the other hand, was as crippling to urban development as Hamilton's utilitarianism. Suspicion and distaste kept the agrarians—the champions of liberty, democracy, and individual independence—from grappling with the realities of city life and the dangers of growing corporate power.

Equally important, no group in the country had more need of government access and institutions to guard their rights than the mass of immigrants flooding the cities. Yet there was no group in the country the Jeffersonians viewed less sympathetically. By default, Hamilton's outlook "guided" urban development. A man of extraordinary vision who advocated urban planning before the phrase was coined, Hamilton did not, however, conceive of cities as having a legitimate public life of their own, as being places that people would call home.

Our cities, therefore, were born in the central paradox of the American dream. To Jefferson, industrial hegemony was irreconcilable with democratic principles. To Hamilton, "pure" or mass democracy was irreconcilable with the nation's attaining the power it had to have to govern and to protect its citizens' rights, particularly their property rights. The two men fought bitterly in their lifetimes; and they left the cities the legacy of becoming battlegrounds for essential themes in American life: Could a state powerful enough to protect its freedoms in the world coexist with individual liberty at home? Was liberty defined as the right of private capitalists to function as they pleased or did liberty include public controls decided by democratic representation? Could a democracy founded in agrarianism adapt to the reality of industrialism?

Paterson was not designed as a city; it was designed as a corporation. While a city's prosperity contributes to its success, wealth is hardly enough as Paterson's history clearly shows. In the almost two hundred years of its existence Paterson has been substantially destroyed three times—once at the height of its material splendor. From the beginning the city failed to offer those other resources—responsive government, public facilities, a sense of community—which were essential to its survival in the long run.

Although Paterson dates its founding in 1791, significantly it was not the city itself that was chartered that year. Instead, the New Jersey legislature incorporated the Society for Establishing Useful Manufactures (SUM), the company Hamilton organized to build and operate the industrial complex. On May 18, 1792, the SUM's directors resolved to locate their enterprise "upon the waters of the River Passaic at a distance not more than six miles from the same on each or either side thereof between the seat of Mr. Isaac Gouverneur near the town of New Ark, and the Chatham Bridge," where they could utilize the falls as a power source.* Among the sixty-five original stockholders (Hamilton was not one) were men who at various times in their careers represented two governors of New Jersey, two Supreme Court Justices, four senators, and nine congressmen. In retrospect, they appear amazingly free of a sense of conflict of interest. The charter, approved by the legislature, gave SUM vast financial and governmental privileges. The corporation and its property were tax-exempt except for having to pay state taxes after the first ten years. SUM could govern its own lands, condemn other property for its own use, and hold lotteries to raise revenue. It also had exclusive domain over the Passaic River or, in effect, the drainage rights to almost the entire water supply of North Jersey. At Hamilton's suggestion, the directors named the town after William Paterson, then governor of New Jersey and a stockholder in SUM.

Even more indicative of the pattern of American industrial-urban development, the charter made no legal provision for the city of Paterson. In his original plan Hamilton—ever haunted by fears for government stability—wanted the board of governors (directors) of SUM to appoint the mayor and lesser city officials, for life; minor officials would name

* *The Minutes of the Society for Establishing Useful Manufactures.* Available at the Paterson Public Library.

their own successors and SUM would always appoint the mayor. Hamilton was advised that the New Jersey legislature, already under heavy criticism for allotting SUM so much power, did not dare proceed further. Consequently the first industrial city of the world's great democracy had no local government for the first forty years of its existence. Not until 1831, after lengthy agitation from the city's residents, did the legislature finally grant Paterson a town charter.

To lay out both the industrial area and the city, Hamilton hired Major Pierre L'Enfant, the engineer-architect of Washington, D.C. Reflecting his patron's bold economic aspirations, L'Enfant said his plan for Paterson would surpass anything yet seen in the United States and would make it the largest and most elegant city in the nation. Nevertheless, his volatile temper and his extravagance delayed the work, and he did not attend to the most mundane yet vital feature of the manufactory—a canal to conduct water for power. As a result, SUM fired him two years later, marking the end of overall city planning in Paterson. It is uncertain if he ever managed to complete a map for the city, although for a time he was remembered by a bend in the river known as L'Enfant's Gap until it was filled in for a roadbed.

In this same period, SUM encountered financial disaster when William Deur, the president of its board of directors, landed in a New York City debtor's prison. The energetic, charming Deur was a wealthy New York speculator and an intimate of Hamilton's, well-connected to the tight New York financial aristocracy. A charming host who "served not less than fifteen different sorts of wine at dinner," * according to one delighted guest, he was also a man whose financial misdealings were so extensive that their exposure precipitated the Panic of 1792, the United States' first depression.

* *The Life, Journals and Correspondence of the Reverend Manassah Cutler* (Cincinnati, 1888).

In early 1792, Deur had formed a secret partnership with Alexander Macomb, another director of SUM.* Their object was to make a killing in U.S. notes through the usual stock manipulation scheme of buying up securities, creating a run, and then selling out at inflated prices. It seems certain that $10,000, which SUM had entrusted to Deur to procure print cloths and workmen from Europe, formed part of the original capital for this venture. With Deur's other connections, he was also able to borrow heavily, and in the space of a few months had created an extraordinary stock speculation fever in the United States. His actions came under scrutiny and in March the Treasury Department instituted a suit against him. The bubble burst, creating chaos in the nation's finances. As for SUM, the panic "shook it to its foundations and threatened its absolute downfall." † Many of its other directors had joined in the speculation and they were wiped out. More important, the fact that SUM's directors were so closely connected with this scheme had ruined its credibility and it became the focus for bitter popular criticism.

Hamilton made every effort to save his experiment from the debris. He privately intervened with the Bank of New York to secure loans to keep SUM going and also tried to straighten out its management and planning problems. Most of the directors had been attracted to SUM in hopes of a quick stock profit, but none had had any experience in industrial management. Finally yielding to SUM's endless difficulties, the directors called a special meeting for October 1796, "to take into consideration the propriety of dissolving the said corporation agreeably to the law in such case." ‡

---

* Joseph Davis, *Essays in the Earlier History of American Corporations* (Cambridge, Mass.: Harvard University Press, 1917). Reissued by Russell and Russell, New York, 1965. Vol. I, pp. 278–84.

† Davis, *Essays in the Earlier History of American Corporations,* Vol. I, p. 409.

‡ *The Minutes of SUM.*

The "national manufactory" then included a cotton mill, a printing and bleaching mill, and had also produced some small articles such as candlewicks. Although SUM abandoned these factories in 1796, the corporation never officially dissolved, probably because a quorum of directors did not bother to attend the meeting.* Paterson's population fell from 500 to 43 and the city seemed destined for obscurity.

Going out of business in four years and helping to cause America's first depression was hardly an auspicious beginning for SUM. SUM's early history suggested the kinds of problems that could develop from an urban-industrial complex built on privilege and lacking in public accountability. However, despite the directors' panic, the charter, with its tax exemptions and water rights, remained one of the single most valuable documents in the United States. In 1809 Roswell Colt, the second son of Peter Colt, a Connecticut builder SUM had hired to replace L'Enfant, became governor of SUM and revived it. Colt immediately grasped the virtues of the Hamiltonian system and was soon one of the richest men in the United States. The War of 1812 cut off manufactures from Europe. Paterson had its factories already built and Colt encouraged the cotton mills, which set the city on a boom.

Until 1900 Paterson was the fastest-growing city on the East Coast, its population increasing an average of fifty percent every decade. Yet the city had no means to handle the social strains of this growth. The tendency today is to wonder what "suddenly" happened to American cities; leafing through the newspapers of early Paterson is not much different from reading them now. The city's corruption surfaced from the time the local tax collector in the 1780s faithfully gathered taxes and failed to turn them over to the federal government. The Passaic Falls straightaway provided a fa-

* The minutes of this meeting are missing.

vored spot for murder and suicide. In fact, Paterson in its
early years could best be described as a Wild West outpost
of industrialism—a violent, rapacious, dirty place. Lacking
cohesive institutions, it bred a passionate, frontier-like character, which is still so ingrained that a recent head of the
city's Community Improvements Department referred to his
domain as Dodge City.

For a time, however, Paterson's erratic nature, in a way,
did contribute to the city's greatness. It became a magnet
for men with ideas as raw as the city itself. In Paterson
people did not just invent; they tried everything—a repeating revolver, a submarine, an airplane that could fly across
the Atlantic. And Paterson did not just manufacture; it produced articles that redefined the limits of life. It is impossible
to think of any other city whose products cut so deeply into
the texture of the United States and not only transformed
its national character, but revolutionized American relations
with the world.

Samuel Colt, inventor of the repeating revolver, exemplified the city's appeal to inspired adventurers. He first
tried to raise money for a factory by roaming the East Coast
with a portable magic show. Finally finding backers in Paterson in 1835, he built The Gun Mill there. Next, he tried
every means, including bribery, to wangle government contracts for his invention. The Army held a demonstration
at West Point and concluded "the arm is entirely unsuited
for the general purposes of the service." * In desperation
Colt even managed to secure an appointment with President
Andrew Jackson, confident that "Old Hickory" would recognize the revolver's importance, but Jackson, in the last
days of his term, didn't have time to meddle with war ma-

---

* Jack Rohan, *Samuel Colt: Yankee Arms Maker* (Finch Press, 1935).

chinery. The Gun Mill eventually failed, but the weapon that would change the settling of a nation had been born.

In 1869, as an entire nation listened by a newly erected telegraph line, a golden spike was pounded into the Utah desert, completing the first rail link between East and West. The railroad engine from the East which made a historic bump against its counterpart from the West was "Engine No. 119," made by Rogers' Locomotives Works in Paterson. Rogers' Locomotives started when "The McNeill," the first engine for the Paterson and Hudson Railroad, arrived from England in 1835. Since no one knew how to assemble it, it lay around in parts for weeks. Thomas Rogers, a carpenter, was among the tourists who came to view the curiosity. He decided the English were not the only people who could make something like that. It took him two years and he nearly abandoned the effort, but with the support and encouragement of several other people in Paterson, "The Sandusky," one of the first American-built locomotives, rolled out of his factory. Until the close of the century, Paterson produced eighty percent of the locomotives manufactured in the United States.

In 1878 John Holland, a school teacher, built the first practical submarine. The submarine, barely large enough to hold one man, had its trial run on the Passaic and was used by the major belligerents in World War I. Holland, an Irish nationalist, made the submarine expressly to "blow the English Navy to hell." The British, however, became chief purchasers of the new weapon. Almost fifty years later, in 1927, an engine made at the Wright Aeronautical Corporation took Charles Lindbergh to Paris on the first solo Atlantic flight. For the second time, a product of Paterson was a source of wild and tumultuous celebration throughout the nation.

The marvelous instinct for showmanship, the raw courage, that characterized the city's inventiveness also showed itself in purely human endeavors. In 1827 "Leaping" Sam Patch, a cotton-mill foreman, decided on a drunken impulse to crown the festivities marking the completion of the first bridge across the Falls by jumping into the river from the highest cliff. The whole town attended the ceremony; the mill workers even received a half-day holiday to watch the wonder of a bridge being put into place. The town constables, getting wind of Patch's plan, tried to find and stop him. As the bridge slowly moved on pulleys to its connection at the other side of the Falls, the crowd let up a tremendous cheer, followed by a stunned silence. A rolling pin fell from one of the guide ropes and all waited for the bridge to collapse into the swirling waters below. Instead, Sam Patch came shooting down, landed at the base of the Falls, and swam to retrieve the pin. The bridge was securely placed and Patch, delighted by the sensation he had created, quit his job and traveled around the country with his pet fox, leaping from falls, bridges, top masts, and virtually anything with some water below. Celebrated in poetry as "The Great Descender, Mighty Patch!," he became the only man to shoot the Niagara Falls successfully without a protective device. This impressive career ended when he slipped on the Genesee Falls. His body turned up in a block of ice on Lake Ontario.

On the surface it appeared that Hamilton's dream had been realized. The six-shooter that came to symbolize the character of a whole nation, the railroad that assured the reality of the American continental empire, and the airplane that marked the end of America's privileged isolation from the world by its oceans represented an extraordinary list of achievements for a city whose population has not exceeded 150,000. But neither the productivity, the ingenuity, nor the city's intriguingly raw and independent spirit was enough to overcome the fact that Paterson's significance in America was to be destructive. For while Paterson expanded the frontiers of industry, the city exemplified the tragic results of American urban policies. Some aspects of SUM's charter, such as the tax exemptions, may be extreme by comparison to other cities; but the basic features of urbanization in the United States showed in Paterson from the outset.

Hamilton, by giving industry a special, protected position, introduced a new dimension into the normal conflicts between private and public interests. From the beginning the industrial aristocracy commanded so much of the city's power and resources that, thereafter, they could only regard representative government and public action as a threat. Then, too, Paterson had no means of regulating public life, either for practical matters such as building sidewalks and sewers, or for the more complex job of assimilating new residents. Even when the city finally obtained its own charter, the powers allocated to local government were so minimal as to be worthless. And finally, the general population, the working-class majority, had neither representation in the city's workings nor a "legitimate" means to obtain influence in the long run.

In effectively establishing itself as a force above government and law, the American industrial aristocracy differed considerably from European aristocracy. In Europe aristocrats gained influence through their service to the crown, which, if not public service, did involve those with wealth and education in the problems of government. But in Paterson, where the wealthy commanded such exclusive privileges in their own domains, government, at least in the form of democracy, could not offer them more; it could only potentially diminish them. Government, therefore, was to be ignored, or fought or bought off, but never participated in, even for the purpose of advancing self-interest. When, in

1831, the legislature finally gave Paterson a town charter over SUM's strenuous objections, Roswell Colt unsuccessfully sued to have the new government revoked, arguing that SUM alone had the right to rule the city.

In addition to their hatred of government, the city's wealthy lived in that estranged, somewhat bitter, and peculiarly American world of self-made men. On the whole, they were uneducated first- or second-generation immigrants with little knowledge of American institutions other than the "get rich ethic." John Ryle, a large silk manufacturer, came from a family of seventeen children and worked in the mills of England at the age of five. Catholina Lambert, the castle builder, worked a seventy-two-hour week at the age of ten. They again differed from European aristocracy in their lack of a hereditary sense of *noblesse oblige* or pride in their surroundings. Their driving force was the awesome will of poverty, and Paterson, where the grosser side of the American dream reigned without restraint, bore the brunt. They had no feeling for Paterson as a place deserving their attention and care; instead, they viewed the city as a moneymaking machine, much as Hamilton had established it. Jacob Rogers, one of the most forthright, if mercenary, men that Paterson has ever produced, beat out his own brothers, and by his own estimation, an indeterminable number of illegitimate siblings, for control of Rogers' Locomotives. Declining to donate a small tract of land to a city hospital, he succinctly stated the attitude of the rich: "I don't owe anything to Paterson."

No individual better typified the kind of man who rose to power under these arrangements than Garrett Augustus Hobart. After graduating from Rutgers in 1863, Hobart was for a short time a suburban school teacher and then came to Paterson to read law under Mayor Socrates Tuttle. He quickly established himself by marrying Tuttle's daughter.

Known as a man with a "remarkable ability to come out on top," he established a personal financial empire and is reputed to have been the head of over sixty corporations, including SUM. Yet he kindly revealed his methods to the youth of Paterson. "Success is not hard to attain," he preached. "I believe any young man can succeed if he will rigidly observe two rules. One is to be at all times strictly honest. The other is to be industrious and economical. It has been my practice never to spend more than I made." In 1966, during Mayor Kramer's inaugural dinner, a curious member of the new reform administration stopped to talk with the city's oldest practicing lawyer. "Well, I guess you've seen crooks come and go," commented the young reformer. "Tell me, who was the biggest crook of all?" "Garrett Augustus Hobart," answered the elderly man, who had been observing crooks in Paterson for over ninety years. He recounted an instance of Mr. Hobart's literally shystering widows and orphans.

Hobart was put on the national Republican ticket of 1896 mainly for his financial connections. As vice-president under McKinley, he distinguished himself by the speed with which he performed his duties as president of the Senate. Some observers attributed this to efficiency; most, to boredom. His one noteworthy act as president of the Senate was to cast the deciding vote against granting independence to the Philippines.

Mrs. Hobart was active in her manner. Because of Mrs. McKinley's invalidism, she had to take over much official entertaining. As hostess, she found it disagreeable that the British ambassador should precede the vice-president in the protocol of the day. Hobart arranged for the president to take his wife's arm first at a state dinner, putting a prompt end to that annoying practice. He had "a high regard for the dignity of his office," *The New York Times* noted in Hobart's obituary.

These glories came to an abrupt end when Hobart died prematurely of an illness officially described as "embarrassed respiration." In Paterson it is rather more simply said that the portly vice-president "ate himself to death." There is little doubt that Hobart would have been on the ticket of 1900 had he lived, and he, rather than Theodore Roosevelt, would have become president when McKinley was shot. Except for an accident of appetite, the whole country might have been run, just as Paterson was, by men whose principal concerns were their pocketbooks, their dinners, and their dignity.

Paterson's public life, under these circumstances, was a losing battle. The magnates were determined that the city should have absolutely nothing, a determination carried to such extremes that it appears to have been a form of madness. Paterson received none of the normal conveniences—not even sidewalks—without bitter and protracted fights. Although Roswell Colt used his position to name several city streets after his own relatives, SUM objected to paying its share for street improvements. Paterson's first strike, in 1794, was over the workers' one demand that their children should have schooling. Not until 1907, despite the typhoid epidemics traced to its water, did SUM finally yield to public pressure and install adequate water filters.

But the stance of SUM and the other industrialists was not madness; it was relentlessly methodical. Their monopoly of wealth and power had, indeed, proved "fatal to the existence of American liberty" and they knew it. The citizens of Paterson bitterly resented both their overall situation and details such as having to pay SUM exorbitant fees for the water in their back yards while the city's most valuable land remained tax-free. Afraid that democracy would arise and reclaim its rights, and thoroughly aware that they could not sustain their privileges legitimately, the industrialists sought to protect themselves by blocking every avenue of public action through local government. They also obtained a stranglehold on other public institutions; SUM sent "certain agents" to deal with the courts, the legislature, and other officials. It even payrolled the press to halt critical stories.*

For decades SUM was successful. Every move to stop it failed. The legislature denied all petitions to curb its power and the corrupt courts actually used several legal actions *against* it to extend its official privileges beyond those already contained in the charter. The city, despite the outcry of its residents, took no action.

Nevertheless, there was one detail SUM could not control. The city's population continued to jump an average of fifty percent every decade. The day was coming when the new arrivals would be aware and vocal enough so that the industrialists could no longer ignore the fact that there were people living in Paterson. The magnates had once guarded their power by stifling local government; eventually their power would depend upon winning the growing forces of "democracy" to their side. In short, it would depend on making big business and bad government an interlocking enterprise. Here, too, SUM would prove to be remarkably successful.

* Robert Herz, *The SUM, History of a Corporation.* Unpublished graduate thesis for the New School, 1939. Available at the Passaic County Historical Society.

> *Dependence begets subservience and venality, suf-*
> *focates the germ of virtue, and prepares fit tools*
> *for the designs of ambition. . . . Generally speak-*
> *ing, the proportion which the aggregate of the*
> *other classes of citizens bears in any state to its*
> *husbandmen, is the proportion of its unsound to*
> *its healthy parts, and is a good enough barometer*
> *whereby to measure its degree of corruption.*

—THOMAS JEFFERSON

The tendency of the nation's founders to view American social organization in terms of country versus city, democracy versus tyranny, and individual integrity versus "the degenerate mob" laid the basis for a form of oppression that has been as fundamental—if less remarked—in the course of American development as slavery. The Hamiltonian capitalists had at least some use for the cities; but, ironically, it was the democrats among the Founding Fathers who sowed the seeds for the most blatant failure of American government. Their emphasis on individual rights was meant to protect freedom; but it produced a system of law so steeped in a strict concept of private prerogatives and so antagonistic

49 ☐ ☐ ☐

to the special protections required by urban groups that mass exploitation was permitted in the name of the liberties of a few. The federal system emphasized states' rights as the means to protect the public from oppression by a centralized government. Yet by making no provision for the government of its cities—except what the states might deign to grant—America left the urban masses, without defined representation and defined rights. In short, the cities had no role of their own in American life and urban residents had no role in their own cities.

As another part of their legacy, American cities were given the difficult job of taking the tired, the poor, the sick, and the hungry from every quarter of the globe, and later from every sector of the country, and turning these "huddled masses" into a cohesive society. It was not a task that would have proceeded smoothly under any circumstances. Yet American cities were also held in lower esteem in their own country than any cities in the Western world. How could American cities turn their citizens into a cohesive society when they themselves were not a cohesive part of the American structure? Initially their outcaste status was a perhaps calculated, but nevertheless benign oversight in the federal system. In the late eighteenth century no one really noticed the cities; they were not significant in the assumptions about American life. Soon, however, people did begin to think about the cities, and when they did, their outcaste status changed to become deliberate exclusion.

Having made no provision for its cities, the United States soon faced the wracking upheavals of the industrial revolution. Europe, too, faced these upheavals, but under terms which led to a far different outcome in the nature of urban life. In the Old World, cities were already established, proud centers of government, commerce, and culture. There the politics of industrial control was confined to a fight be-

tween labor and capital. In the United States the fight
between labor and capital spilled over into an effort to suppress the cities—the raw, alien trespassers on the American
landscape. Everyone cooperated. Rural legislators disliked
and feared the cities. Urban legislators, under pressure from
the industrialists, tried to limit the power of the working
class. Paterson, a city without local government for nearly
one-fourth of its history, and later with so little control over
its own affairs that it needed a special act of the state legislature to install a sewer system, exemplified the result of this
suppression.

The problem, then, for Paterson and other cities was
not only industrial domination but their own inability to
develop a responsive civic structure. With the few pretenses
to self-government that Paterson had been allowed, the city
politic was as estranged from the city public as were the industrialists themselves. The hostile indifference of the great
families and the shifting population of disenfranchised immigrants left a vacuum in which the local leaders were free
to move as they pleased. As long as they didn't get in the
industrialists' way, no one could call to account the small
club of aldermen, ward leaders, judges, and minor officials;
they naturally took great care to protect themselves from an
accounting. The city performed endless favors for the industrialists, from letting them build wherever they chose to
putting the police at their disposal to break up strikes.

More important, local government developed as a force
separate from the community, representing nothing but its
own interests and administering little but its own ends. It
had so few bonds with the public that it became a kind of
private enterprise in its own right. Paterson received its town-
ship charter in 1831. That very year the town treasurer neglected to account for public funds as required by law. The
first aldermen, elected when Paterson was incorporated as

a city in 1835, promptly agreed on the need to distinguish themselves from lesser citizens by wearing badges on their hats to denote their status. (This provoked so much ridicule they had to abandon the practice.) Nothing better illustrated the extent of government insularity than the official response to the cholera epidemic of 1832. In reply to demands that it clean out the disease-spreading cesspools and garbage-infested alleys, the Town Committee announced that it did not have the funds. (The town treasurer had neglected to account for the entire municipal budget that year.) The deaths resulting from the epidemic were discounted as personal presumption. "It seems strange to us," *The Paterson Intelligencer* editorialized, "that [people] cannot abstain from a little indulgence in eating and drinking when a fearful epidemic is in our midst, and when they must know that most of its victims have been those who have given away to their appetites."

Moreover, when the working class did start to build a power base, it was unceremoniously cut off. By 1907 the longtime practice of city aldermen's selling jobs on the municipal payroll was so blatant that the New Jersey Legislature established a special form of government solely for the city of Paterson. It revoked the aldermen's power and left them only such insignificant duties as licensing dogs, peddlers, and junkyards. The mayor became the single elected official with authority; and he appointed everyone from the municipal judge to the education, finance, and police commissioners. Although the aldermen's corruption instigated the change, the result was clearly meant to halt the burgeoning influence of ward politics, then beginning to raise the specter of a public voice in cities throughout the United States.* The mu-

* George James, Series on the Government of Paterson, *The Morning Call* (Paterson), October, 1966.

nicipal reorganization—so reminiscent of Hamilton's original plan—left Paterson with a government commanded by one man, a government without room for dissent, opposition, or choice. It was the kind of government that found the city in the mid-1960s, with a population nearly one-half minority group, without a single black in an important position. That this restrictive charter was judged unconstitutional in 1972 is little consolation for the sixty-five years it was that much easier to keep Paterson subjugated.

For Paterson as a city, however, the critical factor in the long run was not the greed or corruption of the industrialists and the government, but the status of public life and the general population. Every "legitimate" avenue of public expression was closed; the ballot, the press, the courts, all the natural places for action and redress in a democratic society, did not exist for Paterson's residents. The working-class majority had no means of joining the city's life or controlling the conditions under which they lived. Property, citizenship, and sex qualifications restricted voting. In the election of 1850, for example, with a population at 11,300, only 536 people voted. Unions were illegal. During times of labor unrest, the papers featured long columns praising what one once called the latest "most noble action" of the employers.* (If the occasion required, the papers also told outright lies. In 1868, in answer to complaints about SUM's tax-free status, the *Daily Guardian* replied that SUM paid full taxes.)

A public accounting was inevitable. And it was inevitable that it would be violent and destructive while all other

---

* "This was a most noble action and more noble still, inasmuch as it was not asked by his hands," *The Daily Guardian and Falls City Register* of March 3, 1868, wrote in praise of Elias Colt's raising his workers' wages. But Mr. Colt's hands had asked for something, and the workers clearly were not impressed by his nobility because they went on strike two weeks later.

doors remained closed. The tragedy of Paterson's residents was not that they were poor and overworked. Most of them were that before they were drawn to America by the hope of a new life and found, instead, that their place was in a mill on Colt Street in Paterson, New Jersey. The tragedy was that they did not belong anywhere; they had lost the associations and customs of their old countries and yet had no means to integrate themselves in the life of their new country. The tragedy was the distance between promise and reality—the distance between poets and assassins.

As early as 1835 Alexis de Tocqueville, in *Democracy in America,* noted the potential threat from American urban conditions.

> The lower ranks which inhabit these cities constitute a rabble *even more formidable* [italics added] than the populace of European towns. They consist of freed blacks, in the first place, who are condemned by the laws and by public opinion to a hereditary state of misery and degradation. They also contain a multitude of Europeans who have been driven to the shores of the New World by their misfortunes or their misconduct; and they bring to the United States all our greatest vices, without any of those interests which counteract their baneful influence. As inhabitants of a country where *they have no civil rights* [italics added], they are ready to turn all the passions which agitate the community to their own advantage. . . . Disturbances of this kind [riots] are unknown in the rest of the country, which is not alarmed by them, because the population of the cities has hitherto excercised neither power nor influence over the rural districts.

Tocqueville considered urban unrest "a real danger which threatens the future security of the democratic republics of the New World" and predicted they would "perish" unless something were done. He suggested an armed force always at the ready to handle the "excesses" of the town populations.

Before movies and television, a popular entertainment in Paterson was to walk down to the station in the evening and watch "the immigrant train" come in. The city's new residents seemed to arrive at night, as if, almost unconsciously, they knew their fate. Many still wore their native costumes, providing a colorful and interesting spectacle in a city where public hangings were about the only other community diversion. In a curious way, this scene symbolized the future of the humble, confused, but hopeful arrivals; they would always be the outsiders in the darkness.

In a country whose vision of democracy had presumed that individual independence would be protected by an agrarian economy, the industrial working class was considered an outcast from the political and social structure; workers were often regarded as without right to human consideration. A state court, ruling against a strike at the turn of the century, expressed this view exactly. It held that labor was "a commodity" and "no one has the right to interfere with the free flow of commodities."

The mills, the red-brick buildings where people produced commodities and became commodities themselves, still stand in Paterson, but most are abandoned now. The looms are no more, their noisy, awkward machinery long vandalized or sold for scrap. Vines, weeds, and sometimes whole trees have grown through their stark walls, the walls unadorned except for small slits, outlined in a contrasting brick pattern, left for windows. And yet the legacy of the hundreds of stories enacted behind those silent walls, the unrecorded lives crushed and buried and forgotten, is desperately alive in Paterson and other American cities. The pattern of alienation, of public and private failure, of corruption and violence that was established then is as uncompromising as the regular pattern of slitlike windows that served as the only concession to human necessity in the mills.

There were warning signs that Paterson's residents were dangerously—violently—estranged from themselves and their surroundings. Fitful strikes, too unorganized to succeed, were also too furious to be stopped and between 1850 and 1914 Paterson was the most strike-ridden city in the United States. Vandalism was rampant. Anything accessible and associated with either the city or the employers showed the marks of revenge. In 1872 silk manufacturer John Ryle deviated from the path of public neglect and donated a park to the city. The inscription over the entrance read "A Pleasure Provided for All Should Be Protected by All." According to one account, "the vandals" set to work immediately. "They pulled up the flowers, overturned the vases and urns, chipped pieces from the statuary, cut branches from the trees and behaved in a fashion that soon showed their utter disregard for the aesthetic by denuding and polluting the very place intended for their elevation and refinement."

The wide support for anarchism at the turn of the century indicated the population's general state of mind. The people were ready for a cause and prepared to embrace it with a fanatical passion. In 1900 Angelo Bresci returned to his native Italy and assassinated King Humbert I. A group of 1,000 anarchists met in Paterson to express their congratulations to Bresci. (It was said that he had won the "honor" of killing Humbert by drawing lots with several other men.) Ernestine Cravella, a young associate of Bresci, exemplified the spirit ready to burst in the city. After being fired from her job as a weaver, she refused numerous offers from promoters who wanted to display her around the country. She felt that anarchism was "too sacred and too great" to debase it by going on the stage, even to earn money for the cause itself.* Although Paterson anarchists had nothing to do with President McKinley's assassination a few years later, they held a grand ball to celebrate the event.

Finally it happened. The people without representation and without courts, the people left to die of cholera, and the people who were commodities in the "material power of the state," the people who arrived and remained as outsiders in the darkness, seized their world for themselves. The Great Strike began on February 25, 1913, and when it was over, the proud "Silk City"—from its back-street tenements to the castle on the hill—lay broken. Paterson was under a full siege for five months, with gangs of workers and police roaming the streets and attacking each other. A total of 2,837 men and women were arrested. The children were sent to live outside the city—first as a dramatic gesture by the strikers, and later because there was no food.

The strike began as a weavers' protest against new looms that would have cut the number of mill jobs in half. However, bargaining over specific issues was forgotten as it mingled with the outrage of decades of resentment. "Big Bill" Haywood, fresh from a string of victories that had raised socialist unionism to the strongest position it had yet held in the United States, came to head the strike. The leader of the International Workers of the World wore his famous black sombrero and "his one good eye glittered defiance." † Toward the end, with the workers near starvation, and knowing they had lost, the I.W.W. still commanded a crowd of 10,000 at its meetings. "The men, women, and children in that

The handwritten marginal note reads: The Great Strike Feb-July 1913

---

* *The New York Times,* August 3, 1900.
† *The New York Times,* April 30, 1913.

crowd cheered, no matter how bitter were the utterances of the speakers. They cheered indiscriminately remarks that reflected on the courts, the government of the city of Paterson . . . and the American flag," reported *The New York Times*.* Haywood explained it, "The strike is our life." After bleak years of being fined fifty cents for opening a window or laughing while at work, of toiling through the winter in unheated factories and going home to drink SUM's brackish water, of leading lives bounded by rows of looms and rows of tenements, the strike was the first time the men, women, and children of Paterson had felt themselves to be part of something. They would not let it go no matter what the cost.

The employers, accustomed to unquestioned power as their natural prerogative, also had no thought of giving in. Catholina Lambert led their fight from the medieval castle that brooded over the city like a sentinel of divine right. He did not, he said, wish to live in a world where he couldn't fire a man just because he didn't like his face. Lambert mortgaged his entire estate so he could hold out and encouraged others to do the same. The owners refused to meet with the I.W.W. at all and met with other labor delegations only a few times during the five months' siege.

The strike's final collapse left the company owners bankrupt and the workers destitute. The lack of public accountability, and the greed built into Paterson's structure had desolated the city within four years of its founding and desolated it again a century later. Yet the breaking of the industrialists' grip did not signal the beginning of the democratic processes and community participation that might have been hoped for. Three-quarters of the population was foreign-born or first generation, most were penniless, and several

---

* *The New York Times*, May 18, 1913.

hundred women and children had been abandoned by desperate men. It was not a setting for forceful political action.

Moreover, the strike's failure—the months of sacrifice for nothing, the emptiness of broken dreams—unnerved the city. The thousands of disillusioned and poor reverted to hostile apathy, occasionally relieved by absurdly touching efforts to find a solution. Hysterical patriotism was the first balm for the city's grief. When strikes broke out again in 1924, Mayor Colin McLean, at the insistence of the Ku Klux Klan, tried to deport the leaders under the premise that only "foreigners" would cause trouble. The Royal Riders of the Red Robes, a group of naturalized citizens, supported the Klan's efforts to end any "brazen, open, arrogant, and defiant slap at Americanism in this community." The Women's Republican Club reflected the high love of country rampaging through Paterson by announcing its intent to enforce "absolute patriotism." The ladies agreed to knock the hat off any man who didn't salute the flag properly.

A few years later the Chamber of Commerce tried to create an atmosphere of good will by sponsoring a ceremony featuring a specially constructed twenty-five-foot-long hammer. The inscription on its head advised the citizens to "Quit Knocking and Boost," i.e., the city's charms. The point of the day's festivities was printed along the length. "The Hammer, Bury It." The hammer was carted through the streets to great cheers and buried under the site of the present-day Alexander Hamilton Hotel, a few blocks from City Hall. In 1934 a group of prominent citizens formed the "Save Paterson Committee," the one attempt at progress in the entire generation between the Great Strike and World War II.

Under these circumstances, with the industrialists' having lost their exclusive hold and the workers thoroughly demoralized, the government, that exclusive club of ward leaders, judges, legislators, and commissioners, found itself in an advantageous position to take a greater share of the spoils. The tyranny of the political machine began to replace the tyranny of the industrial machine.

As usual in Paterson, SUM's method of dealing with the world confirmed the new order. Like American industry as a whole, SUM originally lived above the law because there were few rules governing the conduct of corporations. Now, however, it faced growing government intervention. Beginning with Theodore Roosevelt's administration, increasingly restrictive legislation appeared on the national level. Labor was gaining political strength and as labor consolidated this power, it also won protective legislation. Although local governments were often corrupt and unrepresentative, they, too, had inevitably increased their power, and enforcement of state and federal laws often depended on the kind of pressure that developed locally.

Moreover, SUM, like much of American industry, had developed a habit of operating outside the few restrictions placed on it. In 1894, by some questionable stock maneuvers, a parent company, owned chiefly by the J. P. Morgan Company and the First National City Bank of New York, took over SUM.* The company formed a water-supply system for all of North Jersey, using SUM's right to "the undiminished flow" of the Passaic to claim every river in the area that fed into the Passaic. It also claimed tax exemptions for several million dollars' worth of property outside Paterson. These actions were illegal. SUM could only use the Passaic for power; the charter specifically forbade it to "deal nor trade except in such articles as itself shall manufacture." That

---

* Herz, *The SUM, History of a Corporation.* Unpublished graduate thesis for the New School, 1939. Available at the Passaic County Historical Society.

SUM did not "itself manufacture" every drop of water in North Jersey hardly mattered as long as SUM could get the courts to approve its latest scheme.

For many reasons, then, SUM reevaluated its relations with the governmental sector, observing that the burgeoning influence of government, in which it had once seen the threat of public action, could also be used as a means to protect industry from the public—as long as the right people were running things. Industry now joined government in such a tight arrangement that, in the end, government itself was administering the welfare of corporations. Gradually, also, the task of "oiling" the system—managing people's lives and trammeling public institutions—shifted from the industrial magnates to the public officials themselves.

In the particular case of SUM, Boss Frank Hague, the legendary figure who ran New Jersey from 1920 to 1949, took up the arrangements. Hague's reply to critics who complained that his methods were illegal was "I am the law." Starting out as a boy who left school to work in a machine shop, he became a multimillionaire merely by finding two convenient spots on the public payroll: as mayor of Jersey City and as Democratic national committeeman. As mayor, he controlled the state through the Hudson County machine; as committeeman, he allocated all federal patronage. The two positions neatly synchronized the growing relationship between political clout and federal order in regulating corporations.

The state also fell in line. In 1933 Charles Roemer, a former Paterson city attorney, filed suit to have SUM dissolved by attempting to have a jury decide whether or not SUM had violated its own charter. A judge who was a former chairman of Hague's machine blocked the jury trial.* At last,

* For a full account of this trial, see J. L. Brown, "New Jersey's Giant Cancer," *The Forum Magazine*, August, 1939.

in 1936, Roemer managed to obtain a hearing before the New Jersey Supreme Court. The Chief Justice, formerly Hague's personal attorney, gave him thirty minutes to present his case and cut him off in midsentence when the time was up. SUM's lawyers were allotted an hour and won.

The corruption involved here was more harmful to the premises of democracy than was the old method of payoffs and mutual forebearance that had once guided relations between government and industry. SUM was now striking at the heart of the American system by aiming at the electoral process itself. For example, an assistant Passaic County prosecutor who grew up in Jersey City describes how, as a boy, he learned his lessons in the American way. His parents, both immigrants, owned a small grocery store. "If my parents hadn't gotten down to the polls, say, by four o'clock on election day, a black limousine with two men inside pulled up to the store. One man would get out and say to my father, 'All right, Mr. Goceljak, time to vote.' So my father would get in the car with him while the other one waited with my mother. Then, when he got back, it would be my mother's turn. The men were always very polite. But, of course, you voted like you were supposed to."

In its new relations with industry, however, the government had just started to realize its potential. This era of cooperation was only a prelude to that era when government would become big business and destroy urban life under its own steam.

Aside from the new dependence of industry on government's good graces, two national events contributed to the machine's growing power: Prohibition and the Depression. With the advent of Prohibition, Paterson, like many other cities, watched without protest as bootlegging racketeers simultaneously exerted their influence over local government.

Of course, the hoodlums did not disappear when Prohibition ended. They stayed to run the rackets and the heroin trade —and to further their part in government, which, with the initiation of large-scale government spending during the Depression, now could provide attractive economic incentives of its own.

World War II brought a sudden revival of industry, nudging the city out of the torpor that had held it since the Great Strike. Older Patersonians now tend to look back on the war years and the period up until the early 1950s as the city's time of renaissance. "It was a good place to live then," recalls one resident. "Paterson was humming. But even then, you could see what was going to happen. While it was humming, people were draining the city. The landlords were carving up houses into cubicles and there seemed to be no thought about the future." As had often been demonstrated in Paterson's history, superficial prosperity was not enough.

The postwar period also marked for Paterson, as it did for many cities, the final decline of local industry. Wright Aeronautical, for example, went from a wartime peak of 60,000 employees to 5,000 and then moved to the suburbs. In Paterson this passage occurred with particularly appropriate symbolism. The Society for Establishing Useful Manufactures dissolved in 1946. Since 1796, it had broken the provisions of an all too provident charter; it had obviously violated antitrust laws; it had corrupted the government of New Jersey. Yet SUM, as always, was one step ahead, and realizing that the game was bound to end soon, it sold out cheaply to the city.

Paterson never seriously considered the problems of replacing industry with the economic alternatives at its disposal. The city was ideally located to become an office and service center for the burgeoning North Jersey area; but Paterson rarely pursued the ideal. Once nicknamed "The Silk City," it was now known as "a wide-open racket town," and the atmosphere of corruption, with the tentacles of the past reaching into every corner, was stifling. Who would fight for the future in a city so shackled by history? Who hoped for progress when urban renewal floundered while politicians squabbled over their stakes in the millions?

Paterson's middle-class citizens started to follow the exodus of industry, and, as the poor moved in, by an almost inevitable process government became Paterson's new business. (Whether this was, as officials often claim, because the public "demanded" programs, or because the officials themselves created more areas over which to have power, the result was the same.) Beginning in the 1950s, programs originating in Washington poured vast sums of money into the till, but they failed to meet the city's needs for better housing, schools, and other basic services. Instead, the tyranny of the machine in Paterson rose in almost direct proportion to its newfound financial hegemony; and there was little difference between the city's being bossed by SUM or HUD (the Department of Housing and Urban Development). In either case, Paterson was being ruled by a conglomerate of initials over which it had little control.

The actors may have changed, but the script for the cities remained the same. To replace Catholina Lambert's building a castle while children worked in his factory, the city planned a $32-million renewal project to benefit business while its Board of Education was so broke it couldn't keep the school bathrooms supplied with toilet paper. To replace Garrett Augustus Hobart and SUM, the city now had the Passaic Valley Water Commission, on which a former president of the City Finance Board under Graves sat as chairman and his former private secretary sat as a commissioner. Blacks and Puerto Ricans found themselves as disenfranchised as previous immigrants. Over half the eligible voters were not registered. Many hadn't registered because they thought it was futile; but many hadn't because they thought it was dangerous. It is not through accident, but through diligence that a city nearing a fifty-percent minority population ends up without a single minority representative in a position of real authority.

Nearly 200 years before, Alexander Hamilton had paused for a cheerful picnic by "the meek Falls of the Passaic." Once celebrated for their beauty and a favorite attraction, the Falls had changed since then. SUM, toward the end of its reign, began diverting 75 million gallons a day out of a normal flow of 87,500,000, changing the cascade into a polluted trickle and the river into what William Carlos Williams called "the vilest swillhole in christendom." But the Passaic Falls were about the only thing that had changed in Paterson. From the day the city was founded, its challenge had been decided. Paterson's failure was not one of simple democracy in the sense of voting and representation; it was a total failure in that the city's structure—its economy, government, and natural resources—had no relation to its citizens.

Just as important as the facts of history are the feelings they leave behind. The past left a distinctive legacy in Paterson—deep-seated emotions, fears, and responses that the city had built up during its lonely decades of neglect.

Connected as it is to the East Coast megalopolis by television, highway, and rail, Paterson retains an amazing individuality. Older residents speak with a distinct regional accent. The city has its own food and drink tastes. No gathering is considered complete without Birch Beer, a soft drink similar to root beer. Every lunch stand and diner advertises that it serves "Texas Wieners." Paterson's Texas Wieners do not come from Texas but are the invention of John Patrellis, a Greek immigrant who thought them up to attract customers to his hot-dog cart during the Depression. There are corners of Paterson which do not seem to have changed in a century. On Lower Main Street, formerly a farmer's market, many of the shopkeepers were born in the apartments above their small stores—as were their fathers.

It is this ability to hold on always to some part of its own that gives Paterson its attractive, haunting quality. Few people, once coming close to the city, have been able to leave it behind. Lafayette returned during his triumphal tour of the United States in 1824. Mrs. Hobart, after scaling the social heights of Washington, spent her last years sitting alone for hours at the museum in Lambert's Castle. Frank X. Graves could easily have claimed higher office after being mayor. Yet he sat out three years waiting only to rule Paterson again.

The essence of Paterson is probably beyond description. It may be the absurd castle or the doomed majesty of the Falls. It is partly an unwritten communal history formed by millions of hours of sweat in red-bricked mills. It is partly the tenements and partly the elaborate Victorian mansions that still dot the city, now often carved into tenements themselves. It may only be what William Carlos Williams called:

> The mystery
> of streets and back rooms—
> wiping the nose on sleeves, come here
> to dream . . .*

Whatever the precise ingredients, the sum of its experiences has left Paterson with a distinct outlook. Too closed off either to assimilate its own residents or to develop a sense of being part of the nation outside its boundaries, Paterson evolved its own way of dealing with the world. All its citizens, white, black, and Spanish, intensely feel the fact of living in Paterson as a separate place. Nevertheless, this communal character is not a unifying force, a shared temperament that binds the city together. On the contrary, between the separate worlds of the workers, the industrialists, and the government chiefs, Paterson's fabric was woven with livid threads of instability and rejection. The city is ridden with confusing and contradictory passions, which are an essential part of its nature, but also make it nearly impossible for Paterson to function. There are two elements that dominate the city's character: a pride so enormous that it sometimes verges on hysteria and a deep-seated mistrust that makes cooperation out of the question.

Paterson has more than self-esteem. The city feels that it is sublimely singular. This egoism partly originates from the same need that sparked the raving patriotism after the Great Strike: people who have nothing must cling to something. It also stems from the emotional response that Paterson almost forces from its citizens. The city's atmosphere has always been electric, charged with urgent struggles—labor, civil rights, politics. Even those who do not get involved can't keep the city from impinging on their consciousness. "Growing up in Paterson, you always had a sense of the city, that it was part of your own reputation," Kramer recalls. "I remember my father. When we went anywhere else, he'd introduce himself by simply saying, 'I'm from Paterson.' I guess the chief example of this was Lou Costello. [The late fat man in the comedy team was a Paterson native.] Whenever he was on the radio or appearing anywhere, he'd always finish by saying, 'Hello to all the folks out in Paterson.' Of course, we'd all be sitting around, waiting for it. . . . If you came from Paterson, you'd say so."

Lurking beneath its touching pride, however, is the city's grating insecurity. As one resident says, "It don't matter, white, black or Puerto Rican, there's no unity. Nobody sees nothing, nobody helps nobody, nobody trusts nobody." One debilitating outgrowth of this insecurity is the frenetic power drive that permeates the city's life. Feeling that the world is somehow against them, Paterson's citizens almost compulsively have to find a place, a bit of prestige, and the protection afforded by power—at any cost to themselves or to the city. As Kramer once stated, "Paterson doesn't need a Mayor, it needs a referee."

With its wounds so near the surface, Paterson cannot bear criticism from the outside any more than it tolerates internal dissent. The city has always found it easier to blame its failures on intrusions from a malignant world rather than to take a painful look at itself. An early historian, investigating how "so wonderful a scheme [as SUM] became, notwithstanding its magnificent prospects, embarrassed," concludes that only L'Enfant, the foreigner, could have been at fault.* "It fell into the hands of a reckless adventurer, a Frenchman." Foreigners, too, leading "the Red invasion," single-handedly started the Great Strike according to a local history written by the senior class of 1932.† "Outside agitators" have been responsible for the recent turmoil over civil rights. "We never had any trouble with our Negroes until all those organizers started coming up here from the South," says one policeman.

* John Whitehead, *The Passaic Valley* (n.p., New Jersey Genealogical Company, 1901), p. 26.
† The Senior Class of the State Normal School, *A History of Paterson*. Privately printed.

Even now Paterson does not feel that it is an integral part of the United States. Of course, it makes the normal gestures—Veterans' Day parades, a belligerent honor for the flag in some quarters, the "Freedom Showcase" in the library—but in reality, America is an abstraction for Paterson. The city simply rejects the outside world as having nothing to offer. In 1903 the Great Fire and the Great Flood virtually destroyed the city. Some 15,000 tourists came to view "the ruins" of Paterson, but Mayor Hinchcliffe refused every offer of aid. "Paterson can take care of her own!" he thundered. To this day Mayor Kramer has encountered fierce opposition in bringing in professionals to run city departments. People oppose the expense, but worse is "the shame of admitting there's no one in Paterson who can do the job," as one old man stated.

For a long time Paterson's pride made it ignore the measures of its decline. The city had a certain confidence—not in the future, but in the past. It seemed absurd to consider that the same forces which had brought Paterson "the genius of an Alexander Hamilton," the Colt revolver, the "Spirit of St. Louis," and "Leaping" Sam also brought it a population of one out of eight on welfare, the second highest number of addicts per capita in New Jersey, and the worst air pollution of any city its size in the country.

If one day might be said to mark Paterson's final loss—its prestige—it would be on the hot August day in 1960 when presidential candidate John F. Kennedy made a swing through the downtown. In 1960 Paterson still retained enough importance to be a must stop on the campaign trail. Eisenhower and Stevenson had come, and the city thronged to these appearances, not necessarily out of enthusiasm for the candidates but to prove that Paterson, indeed, still counted. But Kennedy was the last to show the correct sense that this proud little city must be included in the proper wooing of a presidency. No candidate has ever come again, and as the nation headed toward a New Frontier, Paterson fell to the forces from its past.

4

Uncle Alex, I know you were shot, but I want you to know the city of Paterson is not.

—FRANK X. GRAVES

I see a city on the threshold of greatness.

—LAWRENCE F. KRAMER

William Carlos Williams wrote, "A man in himself is a city, beginning, seeking, achieving and concluding his life in the ways which the various aspects of a city may embody." * Frank X. Graves was, in many respects, a living tribute to this thesis. In 1960, when Graves became mayor, Paterson was in a period of wretched uncertainty. During previous times of trouble, it had at least been possible to focus blame, to berate foreign strikers or the industrialists' intransigence or assign all woes to political corruption. Now the city seemed

* From *Paterson.* Copyright 1946 by William Carlos Williams, 1963 by Florence Williams. Reprinted by permission of New Directions Publishing Corporation.

to be overtaken on all sides by forces—a loss of industry, growing welfare and crime, a failing tax base—it could neither comprehend nor control. What the city craved was some sense of direction, some reassurance of its own importance, and some definition of its life. Graves was acutely aware of this need. For him, Paterson comprised the most important 8.32 square miles on earth and, through his conviction that the city was his own destiny, he was able to infuse Paterson with the sense that it had a destiny through him. Between Graves and the city, there was a kind of magnetic attraction, a feeling that Paterson had at last found its own, which has assumed almost legendary status in the city's memory. "We were all very excited about Frank," Kramer recalls. "Everybody knew he was going to be mayor one day and we were waiting for it. He was an alderman and then on the Board of Freeholders and, whatever he was doing, he was always hardworking and energetic. We expected his administration to be the start of a new era. Sure, he was part of the Democratic machine, but who wasn't? That's all there was in Paterson and he stood out as a man who could get the city moving. As far as Paterson was concerned at the beginning, he could walk on water. That's the kind of response people had to him."

The first factor in his success was that he saw the city in intensely personal terms. He referred to everything in Paterson, people and buildings alike, as "mine," as in "my City Hall," "my TV station," "my police force." Being mayor, to him, was not a managerial problem; policy was not decided by graphs and budget analysis. Instead, decisions were made almost as if the city were his child. He took care of it, but sometimes he had to punish it. He was preoccupied, for example, with enforcing moral standards. He thought it "disgusting" that white men from the suburbs came to Paterson chasing black prostitutes and he personally led

several raids on what he called "the hotbeds of prostitution."
On another subject that drew his attention as he patrolled
the streets at night protecting Paterson, the kindest thing he
had to say was, "Fags! I'll just never understand that."
Surprisingly, he exhibited little racial prejudice—only a good
understanding of who was weakest in his particular world
where strength counted for all. He assessed all policy in terms
of its immediate effect, rather than by overall standards of
good conduct and government.

In addition, he fed the city's pride by fuming against
the federal government, New York's Mayor Lindsay, or any
other convenient object. (One of Lindsay's first communications when he took office—if he saw it—was a telegram from
Graves demanding that he settle the 1966 subway strike for
the good of the people of Paterson who worked in New York
City.) He undertook daring exploits. Disguised as a fireman,
he swooped down on a bookmaking operation on the back
of a firetruck. He strode into ghetto bars and personally
broke up fights. Allen Ginsberg gave a poetry reading in the
city and happened to remark that he had spent a pleasant
afternoon sitting by the Falls and smoking pot. Graves
ordered the police to issue a warrant. Paterson gasped.
Although the city was not thoroughly sympathetic with his
life-style, the poet was, after all, its most famous living son.
Ginsberg sought refuge in New York, and for a while Graves
hinted he would ask Lindsay to extradite him.* (Graves never
did, although the imagined scene of Lindsay's handing Ginsberg to Graves in the middle of the George Washington
Bridge rather makes one wish it had happened.)

Moreover, Graves was like the city itself—a loner taking
on the whole world. He had few personal ties. His mother

---

* Ginsberg's lawyer advised him to wait for a change of administration before
going to court. Kramer's appointee as municipal judge immediately dismissed
the charge on the obvious ground that there was no corroboration.

had died when he was a baby. His father, Frank X. Graves, Sr., an imposing man, quiet and rather stern, was universally described as being "good for his word when he gave it." Graves, Sr., was also a fixture in the city's public life, an elusive elder statesman who had been intimately associated with the city's ruling circles and who knew every secret without having taken an official role himself. Although he had sold his vending machine company for over $1 million, the elder Graves still worked, as he had since 1918, as a police reporter for the *Paterson News* and spent much of his time at headquarters, where a picture of him hung across from a painting of George Washington in the municipal courtroom. There was some speculation that Graves' own preoccupation with the police stemmed from efforts to win his father's approval by modeling himself after the gun-carrying men who had trooped through his childhood. Although Graves himself was a product of the machine, he quarreled with the city's power brokers and ended up on nonspeaking terms with the Democratic county chairman, among others. Graves had little time for his own family life. He was fond of his wife, a quiet, pretty nurse whom he had met when he was wounded during World War II, and of his three teenage daughters. But he often spent his evenings either patrolling the city or holding court with his associates at one of the few selected taverns that became known as "second City Halls."

At the beginning of Graves' term, Paterson, to some degree, thrived on this treatment. The city felt it had found what it needed—a mayor who made it feel somehow secure in its own right and strong enough to face the world. Graves created a continuing sense of excitement and activity, a presentiment that great events were in the making. He seemed to have an almost magical way of getting things done; he obtained one federal program by sending a telegram directly to President Kennedy and pointing out that Paterson's county was being rather slow about helping the city help itself. His personal exploits—chasing fire engines and rushing to accident scenes—gave the impression that he was in full command of every detail of the city's life and that Paterson had a mayor who was a man to be reckoned with. On one famous occasion, he sent a squadron of Paterson squad cars to a nearby suburb to search for Tiger, a little dog missing from the home of a woman. Paterson would not have tolerated such behavior in any other public official, but in some ways the city, as Graves was aware, lived vicariously through him. Who among the men who sweated at their menial jobs, couldn't afford to send their children to college, and watched the blacks "rake in welfare" would not secretly have loved to tell off that liberal Lindsay, arrest that hippie Ginsberg, and sweep through the streets like a modern centurion on the back of a fire truck with sirens blaring? Graves seemed to prove that Paterson still had energy, spirit, and daring.

In other respects, however, Paterson did not thrive. Unless Graves personally approved, very little, from small matters such as housing inspection to large projects such as urban renewal, moved forward. He brushed aside criticism and suggestions. "I am the mayor!" became the slogan of his administration. He would overcome opposition by charm if he felt like it. He used other methods when charm wasn't convenient. As the city increasingly became the domain of one man, those delicate processes which enabled it to function as a community and to balance its various interests ceased to work. As a rule, the result was that those projects and purposes of government which interested the machine coterie flourished after a fashion; but the daily, vital services that offered little incentive by way of power and patronage languished.

Graves made the police—or, as he put it, "law and

order"—the foremost preoccupation of his administration. He glorified the department and, on many occasions, flatly declared that "the police force is the city." Critics charged that the police were, in fact, "a private army." Not all the services they performed were as delicate as retrieving lost puppies. Endless reminders to the contrary were in store for anyone who dared step over the line. For example, a patrolman who had openly objected to the department's methods was reassigned to a lonely night beat. One evening two policemen with drawn guns came to pay their fellow officer a visit, apparently to drive home the lesson. He drew his own revolver. "I told them, if they wanted a fight, I'm ready. Let's get it over with right now. I was so mad. I didn't care what happened, if I got killed. They knew I was serious and they left." Even protected by a badge and a gun, a policeman could no more open his mouth than the people in the ghetto who bore the brunt of the "control" operations. "Checking" the bars was one of the favorite devices for maintaining the balance of terror. "I never seen anything like the way they go into those bars," commented one middle-aged man. "They stomp in just like Gestapos. They push and shove everybody. You don't have to treat people like that. I'll never understand. They're supposed to be smart. I mean, they was chosen. They had to pass the test, didn't they?"

Even some of Graves' most ardent supporters occasionally doubted that his martial exploits constituted a prudent public policy. There was even some apprehension that, through his penchant for personally breaking up brawls and disturbances, the mayor would get himself killed. However, like almost everything the mayor did, the omnipresent police presence served several purposes. It satisfied many that a relentless war against crime was being waged, and as long as that primary concern was satisfied, there were few questions about what other activities the police undertook. The city, most particularly Graves' critics and opponents, lived with a constant feeling of being watched. This vague but pervasive atmosphere of fear effectively kept dissent to a minimum. As public pressure and interest declined, the machine was left in an unassailable position to exploit the city's resources without interference.

Another project that enormously interested Graves, for example, was urban renewal. When he first ran for mayor, the city was planning an industrial park that was greatly opposed by the 900 people in the Bunker Hill area who stood to lose their homes. Graves guaranteed that he would halt the project and received every vote in the district. A few months after taking office, he announced that he did not have the power to halt it. The Bunker Hill Industrial Park was supposed to bring the city factories, jobs, and other advantages. For some inexplicable reason, it was soon tenanted mainly by warehouses. It was also so badly constructed that the federal government finally threatened to cut off all funding for Paterson if the project wasn't terminated. Nevertheless, the $4.5-million scheme did produce some benefits. It saw enough money spread around for Passaic County's contractors to buy tickets for the Democrats' $100-a-ticket galas. The Housing Authority, in charge of the project, employed dozens of people from a Housing Authority commissioner's son and daughter-in-law to the Democratic county chairman's brother. The machine, in short, consolidated its power over the gutted homes of the taxpayers.

The administration's enthusiasm for renewal presented a marked contrast to its interest in the preservation of existing housing and neighborhoods. Landlords illegally converted one-family homes into multiple-dwelling units or boardinghouses without the city's coordinating any effort to stop such practices. As a result, problems that were perfectly controllable at the outset mushroomed out of control. For example, schools in areas where there had been no new construction suddenly became overcrowded. "The people are producing more [i.e., children]. I don't control that," Graves explained. The failure was so glaring that the *Paterson News,* which generally supported Graves, presented angry editorials on the subject. "The finger points directly at the City Administration. It is high time Mayor Graves took a serious look at the situation. If he doesn't, someone else will."

In addition to the city's own lack of initiative, it offered no encouragement to individuals seeking their own redress. Homeowners protested in vain against variances granted by the Board of Adjustment. A welfare mother who went to court to complain that she didn't have a working toilet might typically find her case postponed eight times in a year and a half. "Our efforts are being thwarted in the courts and we have no control over them," Graves cried in response to critics. (The municipal judge also had been his campaign manager.) Mrs. Florence Brawer, an energetic housewife who became known as "Paterson's unofficial watchdog," leading investigations of school purchasing and urban renewal, among other things, started her crusade after an encounter with the Building Inspections Department. "There was a violation in the house next door," she recalls, "and I sent them a letter. Their response was totally unsatisfactory, so my husband and I went down there. Then we saw letters from other people with the same complaints. The boardinghouses brought in a transient population with a terrible crime problem and, of course, people weren't going to stay under those conditions. But they didn't want to leave their homes and the city. The city forced them out."

Even with his consummate understanding of the uses of power, however, Graves could not have proceeded in this fashion if the urban structure in which he operated did not support, if not encourage, him. An always interesting question in public life is whether the man creates the situation or the situation creates the man. There are still many people in Paterson who feel Graves did a good job during the first part of his term, but, as one reformer said, "When he realized the extent of his power, something just seemed to go wrong. Of course, we had previous mayors who weren't perfect, but at least they sat in City Hall and did whatever they were doing and let the people alone. Graves did not let the people alone." The potential of the city to interfere with the people had increased markedly during Graves' years in office; the advent of massive federal spending and urban programs at all levels soon assured him economic clout to match his political clout.

The city was as incapable of protecting itself as it was powerless to seek redress from such outside sources as the courts, the state Civil Service Commission, or the federal government's HUD. Paterson's own social heritage—the procession of immigrants, the racial and ethnic conflicts— precluded the serious cooperation needed to fight a political machine. On a more immediate level, the city's peculiar charter, which left the mayor the only elected official of power, cut off attempts at reform from within government. Critics could not gain "official" or legitimate influence and were easily branded as dissidents and troublemakers. (One group of reformers decided that charter revision was very much to the point and collected the 9,000 signatures needed to put this question on the ballot. The city clerk "lost" the petition and that was the end of charter revision.)

Then, too, Graves did not rule alone but as the repre- sentative of an extensive machine whose tentacles spread to the county, state, and federal governments. Although Graves and his fellow power brokers quarreled to the extent that some insiders wanted to oust the mayor as much as reformers did, the politicos kept the city in the supine position that would assure their own survival—just as it did Graves' continuing power. It would, for example, have been inconvenient for the mayor to deal with a forceful, independent black community. This was not a matter about which he had to worry. When the black Fourth Ward managed to oust the white who had been its ward leader for twenty-six years and then threatened further action, the Democratic county chairman quashed this threat to his own organization by simply reinstating the white.

The city had its closest contact with Washington in the area of urban renewal. Pleas to HUD to halt the carnage parading as renewal came from every sector of the city, down to the Greater Paterson Council of Churches. In the face of these outcries, Graves and Housing Authority Chairman John Wegner made a hurried trip to Washington to mend fences. When they returned, the urban-renewal program continued unchanged and HUD kept supplying the millions of dollars that did more to destroy than build Paterson. Was it that urban renewal, with its preponderant constituency of contractors, real-estate interests, and political backing, just continued to follow its established momentum? Paterson never knew the reason. The one thing HUD did not bother to supply was an explanation to the citizens of the city.

Nor was there relief closer to home. A group of women formed the Committee for the Public Schools to investigate alleged misconduct in school purchasing practices. They uncovered various facts: contracts were often not let out for competitive bidding as required by law; supplies were being bought from stores and vendors, not at wholesale or at retail prices, but from double and up to four times their retail values. Among the examples, the Board of Education had paid $190 for one bulletin board; it was buying cups and saucers (presumably for use in home-economics classes) at $4.30 a set. Considering that irregularities were found in the purchase of items from masking tape to bathroom cleanser, it is difficult to assess how many thousands of dollars such practices had cost the city. The Taxpayers Association, meanwhile, delved into the construction of the John F. Kennedy High School. This school, as Graves liked to point out, was the largest in New Jersey. He proudly called it "my school, I built it," and cited it as proof of his concern for Paterson's future generations. The Taxpayers Association wondered if the mayor's references to the building should be taken literally. The building did not meet contract specifications and the roof started to blow off a few years after its completion. Aside from idiosyncracies of construction, there was also the matter of "vandalism"; everything from typewriters to truckloads of bricks disappeared.

For months the Passaic County prosecutor delayed presenting these charges to the grand jury for action. In the face of public pressure, he finally announced a sweeping investigation of school purchasing practices throughout the county, thus shoving aside the specific question of Paterson. Although the grand jury came up with a presentment advising the Board of Education to reform its procedures, no one was indicted. When the construction chief was called to testify, he announced that he had lost all the records. He was later promoted to the job of chief custodian of the schools.

More crucial than specific corruptions and complaints, however, was the city's final loss of identity, that elusive but vital sense people have of being part of their surroundings. During Graves' administration, Paterson started to live on the edge of a furious futility, grasping blindly at some anchor for itself. The city rioted in 1964, long before larger cities with worse poverty caught up to the rioting wave of the 1960s. Graves blamed the riot on "the worst hooligans that man has ever conceived." But the poisonous rage was hardly confined to the ghetto, a fact of which Graves seemed to be aware. This mayor of Paterson customarily carried a pistol; he was not the only person who thought a bullet might one day be someone's solution.

Yet Graves retained his mesmeric hold on Paterson until the end. There was something in him that was an elemental reflection of the city, and even some of the people who worked hardest to remove him from office conceded a kind of grudging affection for him. Many hoped somehow to force or convince him to turn his unique grasp on the city to constructive uses. Mrs. Brawer finally took to following him around with a 700-page copy of the city ordinances and a two-pound copy of the city building code to inform him immediately when his plans appeared to breach those canons. Such efforts were futile. Graves came, as one person put it, from "that old school where you rolled up your sleeves and put your hands in blood to the elbows," from the absolutist tradition that yawned like a granite abyss back to the city's founding. And because he was such a genuine product of the city's ruling class, Paterson belonged to him; he did not belong to Paterson.

Paterson, like many other cities, had never known anything other than the kind of rule Graves represented. The machine possessed the comfort of familiarity; everything was understood. To find another way seemed futile in theory and impossible to carry out. Paterson was wary of opening itself up to the forces of change. The city could sense the conflicts boiling under its surface, the dissent and dissension ready to burst. The future was as threatening as the past was terrible. It was not only that the city had nowhere to turn, but that experience had taught that it ought not dare to turn. In 1966 Graves confidentially prepared to hand his office to John Wegner for three years.

It is difficult to say where Paterson picked up the courage, or even the idea, to free itself. The city had little education in what it should mean to be American; yet it attempted to find the meaning that all the promises from America's heritage had not been able to give it. Another side of the city's character began to surface, the true pride that enabled Paterson to "take care of her own" through fire and flood, the stubborn faith that had seen the immigrants survive. The inventiveness, the spirit, and the perseverance that had made Paterson an industrial prodigy now focused on the greater challenge of the city's very life. Just as Paterson's poets had been early spokesmen for a new humanitarianism, so its citizens began to throw off the tyranny of history. Somewhere behind the broken windows covered with cardboard along Main Street, somewhere in the honky bars where go-go girls danced to jukebox music, somewhere in what was left of the fashionable East Side section where husbands and wives sat behind locked doors and broached plans for moving to the suburbs, somewhere in the urinous rooming houses there remained a feeling. It was a feeling that came vaguely from an eighth-grade civics class, from looking at children and wondering about the future, from sweating and getting nothing but a larger tax bill. Finally it was a feeling that a man should be able to stand up in his own city. This half-realized, often exhilarating idea came to focus on Lawrence Kramer.

Like many momentous decisions in Paterson, Kramer's decision to run for mayor was made with the same cavalier casualness of Sam Patch's first leap or Thomas Rogers' resolve to make a better locomotive. Kramer was then prominent among a group of young business and professional people who were hoping to "improve government from the outside." Most were members of the Chamber of Commerce and other business groups, and their chief concern was urban renewal. At one point in the outcry over renewal, Graves gave them permission to form a Citizens' Advisory Committee, whose advice, he declared, would be "the last word in urban renewal." The committee set diligently to work and made the

front page of *The New York Times* Sunday Real Estate section with a complimentary story on the city's prospects. However, when the committee disagreed with the plans of Housing Authority Chief John Wegner, Graves summoned
Kramer and the chairman to his office for an angry session.
He dismissed the chairman, and the rest of the committee
resigned in protest.

The experience of being berated for a volunteer effort
to help the city shocked the progressive forces in Paterson.
"It came absolutely as a revelation to us that our ability to
bring pressure from the outside was so limited," Kramer
later said. "We'd always had our various committees, we were
always working on one thing or another and we really
thought we were involved. It was a few months later that
the campaign started. There were about seven or eight of us.
It was a Saturday and we were just sitting in my kitchen
having a cup of coffee. Everybody had a gripe. One person
was mad about the schools, somebody else was mad about
urban renewal. Finally, someone said—I don't even remember who it was—'Damnit, we ought to get this city back.' The
more we talked, the more we realized it could be done. It
just sort of settled on me to be the candidate because I'd had
more exposure from having been on the Planning Board and
the Board of Education. The reaction from the other side,
of course, was uproarious laughter."

The quest began officially with a symbolic gesture—a
walking tour through the Fourth Ward, the city's central
ghetto. Ordinarily such an act would have branded Kramer
with the city's right wing, but Paterson was not in an ordinary mood that spring. Kramer's campaign prompted a spontaneous outburst of public feeling that the city, thus far,
had reserved for strikes or riots. Kramer received a mandate
—a profound expression of trust both in the better side of
humanity and government—such as few men in public life

are lucky enough to receive. He inspired not only votes and support, but, in many instances, notable courage and sacrifice. "It was the most exciting time of my life," he remembers. "Everyone was excited. The campaign just took off. Everything fell into place. People just seemed to assign themselves jobs and start working. And they really worked, eighteen hours a day for months. As long as I live, I know I'll never be involved in anything like it again."

Nevertheless, it was not that simple. The decision to "get Paterson back," taken in excitement over a cup of coffee, did not challenge Graves alone. It challenged the all-encompassing system that ruled Paterson. The success of reform did not simply mean that a few people would lose their positions and others, hopefully more competent and sincere, take their places. It would finish the easy arrangements which had controlled the city for decades. It meant an end to urban renewal, to the courts, to the rackets, to the Board of Elections, to the police department, to the construction plums and all the other fruits that urban America provides for those who elbow their way to the table. For many powerful men, their continuing influence rested, if not precisely in Paterson's destruction, then certainly in the city's debility.

The "other side" prepared to put down the outburst as forcefully as if it had, indeed, been a riot. Kramer began to realize that reform in Paterson wasn't to be won only with hard work and public sentiment. Practical realities demanded that he be in a position to assure the victory of his mandate. As he later remarked, "Even when we knew we had won it on the streets, we still expected to lose it in the voting booth." Good luck and a measure of compromise began to enter the picture. Unfortunately luck and compromise have a way of haunting election results. Kramer's decision did not just mean a campaign; it meant—as became apparent too late—a death struggle.

The challenge of reform in Paterson struck three men in particular, who, aside from Graves, thought they either should or did run the city. And their reactions to Kramer influenced a large measure of the luck, hard work, and compromise that enabled him to keep in the voting booth what he had won in the streets.

In the tangled web of Passaic County politics there were no real Republican and Democratic parties. There was a machine with a Republican branch and a Democratic branch, which, as in many places, operated with mutual forebearance. Paterson was a Democratic stronghold. The Republicans did not fight over the city, and the Democrats did not exert much effort in the suburbs, where the Republicans were strong. Neither party had to waste its money and energy on all-out campaigns and the machine was left to divide the spoils without much interference from the electorate; opening the polls on election day became merely a bothersome rite of passage.

Bozzo

Joseph G. Bozzo, the backstage Republican chieftain, had been working his way up in Passaic County for a half century and had been at the top since 1940. A squarely built man, with an unusually smooth and studious face, the seventy-year-old dean of racketeers held no official position in the Republican party—except that he ran it with such an iron hand that many of his associates feared to say his name aloud and circumspectly called him "the Man." Although the Republican party possessed little influence in the city, Bozzo himself was a master arranger with a strong personal following. Wherever there was money to be had or power to be wielded, there also was a friend of Bozzo's. A Graves' appointee to the Finance Board called him "a wonderful guy." An appointee to the Housing Authority referred to him as "my dearest friend." Mrs. Betty Van Dine Smith, his faithful seventy-year-old confidant, was county supervisor of elections, courtesy of a special act of the state legislature. She oversaw the conduct of every election from alderman to congressman —to mayor. Heavy-jowled Joseph G. Muccio served officially as an investigator in the county prosecutor's office, also by special act of the state legislature. Bozzo was his son's godfather. Muccio's activities included harassing the press and assaulting a witness in a gangland murder trial.

Bozzo had two unusual qualities for a man of his ilk. The first was his appreciation for the danger of arousing public opinion. He had no interest in being known as a power and carefully stayed in the background. A story frequently told about him was that early in life he had met with New Jersey's leading mobsters and told them, in effect, that they were going about their business the wrong way. The proper way to get things done was the "nice" way. Whether this was true or not, Bozzo turned from the practices of his youthful associates, who included such figures as Joe Adonis and Willie Moretti, and avoided the nasty headlines, gang warfare, machine gunnings, etc., that were common in New Jersey. When pressed, he would play rough, so rough that one of his victims retaliated by attempting to stab him in a voting booth. However, Bozzo preferred to reach his ends through charm and inducements. "He had a very polite, well-mannered air," remarked one of the few reporters who knew him. "I guess it sounds funny, considering what he was, but he struck you most of all as being somewhat old-fashioned, as if he had just stepped out of the Old World."

Bozzo was extraordinarily successful in avoiding publicity. Only twice in a long and fruitful career did it seem he might be called to account. In 1950 a furor arose when his influence over the governor was tied to $25,000 he had "donated" to the Republicans. Bozzo explained that he personally had not donated the money, but it had been presented as a loan from Lou Costello. Costello, who was Bozzo's cousin, corroborated the story. He said Bozzo had asked him

to loan some campaign money to the Republicans and since
he had $50,000 cash in his pocket at that moment, he had
turned over half of it. On occasion, the simplest explanations
suffice, for the incident was forgotten. The Kefauver Senate
Racket Committe summoned Bozzo to its hearings in 1951,
but again nothing came of it. And such was Bozzo's tact that
he had only been publicly involved in one killing. In 1927 he
beat a man to death on Main Street. It was judged self-defense
and he quietly supported the deceased's widow.

Bozzo's second quality was his genuine interest in politics. He had, of course, discovered that political control was
the most refined technique of getting what he wanted, but
his interest went beyond manipulating officials. He was fas-
cinated by the strategy and excitement of campaigns, moving
the pieces, and outwitting his opponents. Although he had
spent most of his career cooperating with Democrats, he liked
the fact that the Republican party in Passaic County was his
exclusively. For the elderly bachelor, the party was like his
family; he took personal pleasure in nurturing it and watching it grow and wore gold elephant cufflinks on important
occasions. Although he was feared, among the inner circle
that worked the county he was probably the most respected
broker on the scene. His extreme care in avoiding adverse
publicity, his sense of loyalty, his instinct for patience and
strategy had enabled Bozzo to build an operation of extraordinary discipline and thoroughness. A few forgotten headlines, a youthful brawl were all the public knew about him.
Despite his clear power, however, there was only one final
prize in Bozzo's world—formal control of Paterson. This was
the goal toward which all the pieces moved. And Bozzo stood
between Kramer and the Republican nomination.

The Democratic boss, Tony Grossi, was one of four sons
of Carmine Grossi, who ran a small grocery store in Paterson
for thirty years. Three sons remained in the city, all in public

positions. A short, cheerful-looking man, Grossi had once been an announcer for an Italian radio program and he never lost the look or the manner. He wore his graying hair pomaded in 1930s' style and conducted Democratic meetings with the gusto of an emcee who has consolation prizes for all. He was the perfect host, keeping everyone happy with an endless round of Democratic galas, dinners, meetings, affairs, candidates' nights, tea parties, and coffee klatches. His own conviviality and his constant hovering over "the party faithful" made many people in Paterson who had a place nowhere else feel that they counted for something in the Democratic party. But Grossi also knew the brass tacks of his business; he had been Democratic county chairman for a decade. During that time almost every Democratic power in the city, including Graves, had tried unsuccessfully to oust him. Mayors came and went, palace revolts surface and were quashed, reformers rallied and dispersed, but Grossi always stayed.

Beneath its air of public hospitality, the Democratic party worked as an exclusive club. The way Grossi saw it, you had your "boys" and a couple of women so uniquely talented as to be considered "one of the boys" and that was it. In their more inspired moments Tony and his cohorts believed in the Democratic party as that sweaty madonna, the protectress of the working class. However, the only people allowed in the inner circle were those such as "G.I. Jimmy" Vasile, Tony's one-time chauffeur, who once served as county purchasing agent, as an urban-renewal relocation specialist, or anywhere else a trusted man was needed; Fred Ardis, another former chauffeur who quit as county purchasing agent after questions of double-billing arose (the county counsel gave Ardis a clean bill on that matter, calling it "a clerical error," but Ardis was later indicted for fraud in another matter and pleaded guilty to the lesser charge of forgery); John Thevos, the county prosecutor, who had not tried one case in his eleven years on the job; Robert Roe, a former county freeholder who went on to become state commissioner of conservation and economic development, where the prices his department had paid for land came under the scrutiny of a special legislative inquiry which recommended that the department reform its purchasing practices. These were the people who ran the city and the county on a day-to-day basis, "the diadems in the crown of the Democratic party," as Tony liked to call his boys.

Grossi and his circle seemed to be set apart in a world where the endless hustling of ward politics was the sole boundary. The important questions facing the city, issues such as urban planning, civil rights, mass transportation, or drug addiction, rarely entered their deliberations. They had no taste for theory and speculation, and were preoccupied by a relentless pursuit of the specific and arrangeable: life and death, war and peace, all were passing chimeras compared to such questions as who should be placed as comptroller of the Paterson Housing Authority or as an investigator in the prosecutor's office. The result might not have been good government, but Grossi's single-minded determination did succeed in one respect. He had built a party with a strong organization, notable patronage power, and 7 to 1 registration in its favor at the polls. As state senator, Paterson tax assessor, and later a state public-utilities commissioner in addition to being county chairman, Grossi also wielded direct personal power in the city, county, and state. All these strands had been welded into a machine with a remarkable ability to steamroll into office almost any candidate of its choosing.

It seems doubtful that these arrangements could have proceeded so smoothly in the face of public scrutiny. The public, however, did not get an incisive look at them because the third person who thought he ran Passaic County was Harry B. Haines, publisher of the *Paterson News*. A small man with the face of a wizened hawk, Haines, at eighty-six, still went to his office every day and seemed to thrive on the fear he inspired in both his subordinates and the politicos. His paper was a singular combination of the *National Enquirer* ("They Live on Borrowed Blood" read the headline introducing a front-page story about a family of chronic anemics), a constant vigilance against the communist conspiracy and "all foreign 'isms,' " political maneuvering, and bad race relations. The paper did not have one black reporter and consistently editorialized against civil-rights activity. It was the largest-selling newspaper in the county.

Haines had two passions. The first was statues. For decades he had been associated with every piece of public statuary to grace the city and, at one point, had predicted that Paterson would soon be known as "The Florence of America." Haines' crowning achievement was the Plaza of the Gay Nineties, a concoction in Eastside Park. The *News* continually reminded its reading public that the Plaza, "conceived and created by Harry B. Haines," was "the only one of its kind in the country." Aside from the watering-trough centerpiece, gas lamps, and hitching post that were featured as part of its original theme, it also had a Plaza of Memories, a kind of local Hall of Fame. The Plaza's final attraction was a statue in tribute to *Motherhood!* This was not the only statue honoring Motherhood that Haines had donated to the city but it was the one which taught Paterson about Haines' second passion—power.

When the statue was erected in 1950, then-Mayor Michael DeVita had a quarrel with the publisher and subsequently ordered him to remove his plaster from public property. The publisher declined and DeVita responded by sending a sanitation truck to pick up the lady and deposit her in the dump. Haines went into an editorial fury, accusing DeVita of being against motherhood. This was a difficult

charge for a politician to bear and DeVita was eventually
forced to return the statue. But that was not the end of the
incident. Haines worked furiously to see DeVita defeated in
his next election, not to mention the six comeback tries he
made afterward. Subsequently many people called Haines
"the Mayor of Paterson" no matter who officially occupied
the office.

It was a title that Haines coveted. He as swiftly retaliated
against those who thwarted him as he supported those he
favored. The paper kept track of the most minute movements
in the city, took an unusual interest in people's private lives,
and had files on their foibles going back for years. People in
public life in Paterson had learned to fear the *News'* power.
Haines was also closely associated with the tight ruling circle.
If it was necessary to refer to Bozzo at all, the paper usually
described him as "a leading Republican" or, more simply,
as a "real estate man." The *News* featured articles on Graves'
efforts on behalf of the city even while he was out of town
for the weekend. Prominent members of the staff had various
interests, including outside employment as "public relations
advisors" for persons seeking favorable attention. But it was
the aura of power that drove Haines. Although he had moved
his residence to New York City, where he had large real-
estate holdings, Haines held a firm belief in his ability to
decide what was best for Paterson and who should run the
city. He believed in his friends and associates, in things as
they were, and a city that functioned after his prescription.
He had no enthusiasm for seeing reform gain either publicity
or momentum, and had a powerful tool for seeing that this
did not happen.

One by one, all these factors fell in Kramer's favor. The
first break came through the press. The *Morning Call,* the
city's second paper, tottering on the brink of bankruptcy,
changed hands in 1964 to become a liberal, crusading journal.

By the time of the campaign it was churning out steady exposés. "I don't think, in the end, we would have decided to go ahead with the campaign at all if the *Call* hadn't changed," one of Kramer's aides recalled. "It was the final factor that enabled us to try. At least we knew we would have a chance of getting out our story." The *Call* endorsed Kramer twice, once moving its editorial page to the front page so the city could not miss the point.

The second to come around was Joseph G. Bozzo. It was never clear why Bozzo chose to upset Passaic County's traditional arrangements and "go in pitching for Pat," as he put it. Two factors probably influenced his decision. One was his acute sensitivity to public opinion. He had the power to deny Kramer the nomination, but it would have been a costly and nasty business to beat back Kramer's support. More significant, perhaps, Bozzo was exasperated with Grossi. The two held entirely different attitudes toward politics. Grossi feverishly followed the moment; he loved the meetings, the press coverage, the pictures in the paper, and the happy celebrations with the boys. Bozzo took the long-range view, waiting in the background. He did not care about the immediate, because he knew his time would come when others made their mistakes. "I never invested money in politics. I never invested in people," he once said. Bozzo held the advantage of cynicism; he did not invest, he picked up the pieces. Moreover, Bozzo felt Grossi was keeping too much for himself. The two had had a vicious quarrel. If Kramer had not appeared, no doubt this quarrel would have been patched up. But Kramer did appear and, despite the reform label that went with him, he presented Bozzo with the intriguing possibility of shutting out Grossi and clamping Graves. What could the blue-eyed mayor do in any case in a city where Bozzo's cohorts already occupied strategic positions? Bozzo decided to experiment and the Republicans had a candidate.

Grossi presented Kramer with his third break. In his constant efforts to keep everyone happy and in the fold, the county chairman had ironically promised away too much and lost direction of the organization below him. Several prominent Democrats were under the impression that Grossi had given them the nod for an inside track on the mayoral nomination. Other functionaries, chafing against Graves' long one-man rule, had believed that when the mayor's term ended, Grossi would step in and assure them a place in the sun. Graves, however, was not ready to end his rule. He wanted his close associate John Wegner, the chairman of the Housing Authority, to run. Grossi was trapped between Graves and the other claimants who expected satisfaction. But in spite of their conflicts, Graves and Grossi were bound to each other as the two most powerful Democrats in the city. A split between them could only ruin the party. Grossi sensed the danger either way, but he finally opted for the choice he hoped would produce unity and agreed to Wegner.

In the end, the choice of Wegner produced anything but party unity. The fifty-two-year-old bachelor was one of those fascinating products of machine government—the rearguard, a man who carried out his role without complaint or comment. His career had consisted of chairing the powerful Housing Authority for Graves. The criticism of his handling of urban renewal had been vociferous—and later even provoked an "indignation rally" sponsored by the Chamber of Commerce and attended by some 800 people—but Wegner appeared content to let the blame for Graves' projects fall on his own shoulders. Indeed, Graves had once sought to protect himself from the outcry by promising not to appoint Wegner to another term. (True to form, he later named Wegner to another five-year stint.) A bald, heavy man, Wegner did not even appear to have an overriding desire to become mayor, but accepted his role as if it were just another assignment.

Friendly, and unexpectedly humorous in private, he was extremely shy in public and found the campaign trail uncomfortable. He consistently missed campaign appointments, including three scheduled debates with Kramer. But Wegner possessed one overriding asset: he was the lieutenant Graves most trusted not to become independent.

Wegner presented a perfect target for the reformers. More significant, he was a target for his own party. Had Grossi united the Democrats, the party's vast political resources—workers, poll watchers, the election-day machinery —might well have propelled the Housing Authority chairman into office. However, the specter of Graves' retaining power through Wegner and then making a comeback to rule the city for almost another decade, infuriated many of the faithful. They seized this opportunity, not necessarily to reform the party, but to retake a share of the spoils. The Democrats split in a bitter primary that Wegner barely managed to win.

The Democratic split, the general discontent with the choice of Wegner, and the increasing sentiment for reform all pointed toward a conclusive victory for Kramer. Kramer knew Paterson and he did not come to this conclusion. After his legion of workers thought they had thought of everything —even to flying in a voting-machine expert to check out the machines—they learned some things they could not have imagined. In the poor sections of the city, for example, people were convinced that there were cameras in the voting booths and feared retaliation for making an independent choice. The Honest Election League of Paterson reported threats of the loss of jobs, public housing, and welfare. Some union members charged that they could not obtain their paychecks without making a donation to the Democratic campaign. "I can picture the Almighty God standing on top of Garrett Mountain and weeping over Paterson and Passaic County," thundered Monsignor William Wall, the head of the Election League.

There was no weeping on election day in Paterson, New Jersey. The city exploded, in celebration, relief, and satisfaction. Cars roared through the streets all night, and the sound of honking mingled with joyous shouts. On January 2, 1967, Kramer and his entourage—seeking a gesture at once serious and gay—decided to wear formal dress to the inaugural ceremony. Standing on the steps of City Hall, they were a group of happy, sincere, and optimistic men and women. Hilda Conn, the wife of Kramer's campaign manager, typified their outlook. While her husband served as the unpaid coordinator of federal aid and later became city counsel, she plunged in as the volunteer head of summer youth activities. Like the others, she had no previous association with politics. That she, a housewife, bounded by home, husband, and children, had helped defeat a professional political machine and joined the very process of government, confirmed for her and the rest of the new administration a guiding certainty that "the system" could be made to respond. While they knew that honesty and hard work had not yet proven very operative in Paterson, Kramer's supporters assumed that the same hard work that had "won back the city" would also change the city.

Their mistake—simple but crippling—was believing what they had been taught rather than what they had learned. Already the bitter campaign was fading from their minds. They laughingly recalled the shock the voting-machine expert had caused the opposition and all the other anxious, infuriating moments as if these were moves in an old game. However, the system controlling Paterson did not go away courtesy of an election and the structure on which that system had thrived did not change simply because Paterson had decided to stand up for itself. The game was just beginning.

A quarrel between two aging bosses, a newspaper going bankrupt, a few compromises that seemed so minor they were forgotten, the long hours of painstaking work and the hopes of 150,000 people—it was not altogether a solid foundation for a reform mayor. At the inauguration ceremony someone jokingly suggested that, just to be sure, Graves should be sworn out as well as Kramer's being sworn in. (Graves had refused to attend.) In the cold, fresh winter air, young, trusting, and wearing top hats, the Kramer administration enjoyed one of its few happy moments laughing over this suggestion. Graves immediately rented an office across from City Hall where his physical presence could serve as a reminder of where people would be well-advised to place their loyalty. John Wegner still sat as chairman of the Housing Authority and controlled the millions in federal aid on which the city rested its expectations. Joseph G. Bozzo sat back, shuffled his cards, and waited to redeal.

5

Paterson speaks from workshop and mill
For all to forge a better will.
It warns that machines in their glistening pride
Are only mankind magnified,
For the machines themselves but can
Magnify strength and weakness of man.

—LOUIS GINSBERG *

The new mayor appeared to represent the flowering of middle-class America: he was well-to-do but not rich, handsome but not striking, intelligent but not intellectual; up to the moment he decided to run he had lived contentedly in the mold of millions of his contemporaries. Born during the Depression, he was scheduled to leave the hospital on the day Roosevelt closed the banks. The hospital refused to accept a check as payment for his delivery and his father didn't have enough cash on hand. His nickname, Pat, came from the family friend who bailed him out. As the youngest child and

* From "Poem to Paterson," on the occasion of the city's 175th anniversary. Permission courtesy of the author.

only son among four sisters, he had experienced problems but not tragedies. He completely recovered from a case of childhood polio. After high school, he went to Clemson University in South Carolina and married following graduation. His father then planned to expand his small construction firm to South Jersey, and Pat was to move and take over the new branch. However, his father died and he stayed in Paterson.

For the next ten years he followed the routines of a man of his position and time: business, home, family, and enough peripheral public service to be designated a Chamber of Commerce "Outstanding Young Man of New Jersey." His tastes and his social life were straightforward. He enjoyed good food, had a weakness for unusual ties and sports jackets, and spent most of his time with a close circle of friends whom he had known for years. He and his childhood friend Charlie Parmelli still pursued their longtime hobby of restoring antique cars. For vacations, he, Mary Ellen, and a few other couples went to Miami Beach together. "I know it's not very sophisticated," he once remarked, "but, frankly, what we like to do is sit on the beach all day and get lazy and then eat all night and get fat." Outgoing, friendly, and often charming, he also showed on occasion an unexpectedly cynical bent of humor.

But Kramer had decided to run for mayor in an election that was generally expected to be a bloodbath; it was an impulse that he had difficulty defining. "I don't know," he mused, when asked directly. "I guess you just look at your children growing up and start to wonder what you've been doing." He was, further, strongly attached to Paterson as a home and had always held a deep interest in the city. His collection of Paterson "memorabilia" included items such as old street signs and a doorknob from the city hall that burned down during the Great Fire of 1903. After a few months in office, curiosity led him to the City Hall basement "just to see what I might find down there." Among some papers stuffed in an old box, he discovered the most valuable document of Paterson's history—a book containing the minutes of the Society for Establishing Useful Manufactures dating from Hamilton's first meeting with the directors, recorded in the clerk's elaborate handwriting, to the typewritten entries of later years. (The SUM notes are now preserved in the Paterson Public Library.) He was particularly proud that the city's long effort to have the Passaic Falls declared a national historic site was successfully concluded during his administration.

This interest, however, was limited in certain respects. Had Kramer wanted an entry into public life, he could have sought it much earlier. His father, like Graves' father, had been an elder statesman in the city, associated for years with the inner Republican circle, and had served as the chairman of the Board of Public Works in the 1940s. But, unlike Graves, who joined his father's vending-machine company and simultaneously plunged himself into politics right after high school, Kramer and most of his circle were college-educated. Perhaps because they were products of the 1950s, they had found the city's rampaging public life too vicious for personal involvement. Kramer, in fact, was the sole person in the new administration with experience in government. Before the dispute over urban renewal, Graves, required by law to appoint an equal number of Republicans and Democrats, had named Kramer to the Planning Board and then to the Board of Education. Kramer had not used these posts to seek change. "I admit it," he says. "I was a good commissioner as far as Graves was concerned. That is, I was a nice, quiet guy who minded my own business—which is exactly why he appointed me. But you know, people just don't like to get involved. I can't even count the number of good people I've asked to serve on these boards and commissions who have turned me down. They say they're very honored, but they just don't want to open up their lives to all those pressures." Although the city had a few strident reform groups—such as the Committee for the Schools—he had not worked closely with them, preferring to confine his efforts to more traditional organizations such as the Chamber of Commerce.

The limits and experience of Kramer's life had taught him two basic values. One was a quintessentially American belief in "practical solutions" such as new housing and new schools; the other was an attitude of generalized trust. Kramer was not philosophical, but he did assume that people were relatively "good" and that human progress followed in the wake of enough practical solutions. He distrusted both causes and power. Although his own election had been a passionate cause, he did not turn himself (as have other urban mayors) into a spokesman for the plight of the cities or an advocate of radical reordering of national priorities. He thought that people in general could work out their own problems if government would provide an atmosphere of calm and integrity. Some of these attractive personal qualities probably hampered his performance as mayor, for Kramer took office having had little experience with emotionalism or with the darker side of human nature. The deep, wrenching rage of the cities' minorities baffled him as much as the deliberate spite of his opponents. He expected that Paterson would respond to good will and good programs and did not, for a long time, understand that the city was not free to respond to what he offered.

The thrust of Kramer's campaign was a promise to rebuild the city physically, but he was also concerned with its spirit. He specifically set out to make his administration different in tone from Graves'. He desired to restore trust, confidence, and a sense that government was not only responsive but belonged to the people it served. As "an open administration," citizens could easily obtain appointments with their new officials, up to the mayor himself. (This practice was somewhat curtailed after Kramer encountered a few of that particular species who like to "tell it to the mayor," one of whom he thought intended to assault him.) He wanted the city to feel a change inside itself, to be more comfortable and calm. Graves' publicity stunts and endless intrusions dismayed him. "The mayor's job is leadership, not ownership," he noted dryly. He was determined to let people alone. Finally he wanted improvements: "real things that people can touch and see and know are for their benefit, not gimmicks like Graves produced. The newspapers would complain about something and he'd run around for a few days patching up things and that would be the end of it. Government is a full-time job. You have to work at these things steadily."

In its early months the Kramer administration did, indeed, seem to be everywhere. In quick order, the mayor started a senior-citizens program, obtained federal aid for six portable swimming pools and the playground under the highway, initiated summer youth activities, passed an anti-litter law (which no one obeyed), expanded the narcotics squad, changed the police cars from Graves' personal colors of black and yellow to burgundy and white, appointed the first black to an executive position at City Hall and the first blacks to such city commissions as the Board of Education and the Board of Alcoholic Beverage Control. His appointments to head major city agencies were on the whole of high quality and some of these appointees served the city at considerable personal financial sacrifice.

Within six months, the value of Paterson's new spirit became apparent. In July 1967, the city of Newark erupted like a flaming blister. When it was over, twenty-seven people lay dead. The electric spell of destruction rushed across North Jersey. Every city in the area—New Brunswick, Plainfield, Elizabeth, Jersey City—followed in its own measure of violence. Paterson, sick with apprehension, waited its turn. The administration and the entire spectrum of black leadership put together a stunning show of cooperation. The mayor appeared in the streets, held a meeting with some teenagers arrested for throwing bottles to discuss their complaints, and generally tried to head off trouble. The blacks beat back the psychology that said Paterson had to riot because every other city had. One leader, then being touted in the press as the city's "militant," kept stating the city had no cause to riot. "The administration isn't apathetic or indifferent like Newark's," he explained. "It has set up grievance procedures." Much to the disgust of the police brass, the mayor also agreed to the blacks' request to keep the police out of the ghetto. Graves predicted that a riot would result because Kramer had "completely destroyed the morale of the police department."

Kramer still recalls with a wondering smile "the magic formula" he worked out when, three days into Newark's flames, the blacks came to him with the warning that Paterson's day was at hand and demanded he "do something immediately." He and Hilda Conn sped to the Public Works Department and grabbed three trucks. Then they headed to the bars. "We went to some dives, and I mean some real dives. Finally we commandeered three bands. We literally grabbed them and threw them up on back of those trucks. I'll never forget the look on some of their faces." Next they drove down Graham Avenue and put on a huge block party. "We danced those kids and we danced them until they fell over. We didn't stop until they were so exhausted they couldn't have picked up a bottle to throw to save their lives. We were holding this city together with bubble gum."

In April 1968, when machine guns circled the White

House after the murder of Martin Luther King, Paterson was again an exception—an exception made more remarkable by the fact that the city was the last place in the North where King had appeared before his death. Only a few days before, several hundred people had stood outside the Community Baptist Church to listen to his words broadcast over loudspeakers when the small building could no longer accommodate the crowd. Following this second, stunning victory for the city, Kramer made an extensive walking tour. He refused to take the press with him. "I just want to go and tell people how proud I am," he explained.

Nevertheless, all was not well in Paterson. The euphoric sense of belonging that had captured Paterson and seen it through two crises that devastated many nearby cities was an illusion. The city no more belonged to itself than it had when the board of directors of SUM retained the right to appoint the mayor. The state and federal governments, the courts, the Civil Service Commission all stood in the way of progress. Men, both in and outside the government, who were not elected or reachable by public influence, often held decisive power that the mayor himself could not fight. The city's institutions responded, not to the electorate, but to the pervasive structure of influence and power that had controlled them for decades. Kramer increasingly met stone walls in his efforts to gain control of what he had won. He had no tools. He couldn't innovate: a police-community relations program for which he had obtained a federal grant was so well sabotaged from inside the department that the chairman of the Police and Fire Board himself publicly declared the program had "fallen right on its fanny." Kramer couldn't fire anyone: two policemen caused an explosive situation by claiming that three black youths had shot at them. The black youths, in truth, were nonexistent and the wounded officer had shot himself in the leg while playing with his gun. When Kramer fired them, the Civil Service Commission ordered their reinstatement.

In addition to the problems of changing the city's existing institutions, the obstacles to introducing new programs were almost insurmountable. During the campaign, for example, Kramer had released several "white papers" on housing, promising to improve the situation through the dual measures of starting a professional building-inspections' department and appointing a second municipal judge to handle these "social" cases. The mayor placed Donald Herzog, an old friend, in charge of setting up the program. Herzog did such an excellent job that he won praise from some of the administration's most vociferous critics; nevertheless building inspections stumbled. The last step was to hire a trained coordinator. With experts' preferring the larger salaries and glamour of big cities, small cities such as Paterson have great difficulty hiring trained personnel. After a nationwide search, Kramer located Clarence Bechtel, a code-enforcement specialist from Minneapolis willing to direct Paterson's program. The New Jersey Civil Service Commission, controlled by Democrats, declined to confirm his appointment, explaining that it needed time to make up an appropriate test for this new position. A year later it had not scheduled the test. Bechtel, who had left his family in Minneapolis thinking it would only take a few months to settle the situation, quit. Kramer persuaded him to take a leave of absence instead. A year and a half later he was given a test, which he passed.

Kramer's appointment of a second municipal judge also took nearly two years. First, the state legislature had to give its permission. The bill languished in the legislature for a year. After passage, it waited several months for the governor's signature. Governor Hughes, who had spent a full day in Paterson campaigning for the opposition, offered no public explanation for the delay. Kramer's appointee to the one municipal judgeship was holding court six days a week and Wednesday nights to keep up with the caseload. "It's killing me," he allowed and resigned to protest the delay.

Still, the governor did not sign for several more months and, even then slum clearance did not proceed smoothly. In the basement of City Hall Ralph Ventrella, a longtime Democratic retainee, occupied the post of chief buildings inspector. Ventrella held the statutory power to order the demolition of abandoned or burned-out buildings at the owner's expense. Saying that his own inspection showed that the buildings did not need to be removed, Ventrella often declined to issue the demolition orders requested by the Kramer administration. Graves, meanwhile, made a continual issue out of Kramer's failure at slum clearance and sent the mayor a public telegram demanding that the abandoned buildings, which were eyesores and presented a constant danger of fire, be removed. "Kramer should be ashamed, letting junk like that stack up," Grave asserted. "Children play in those buildings and they get hurt."

As reality crashed upon implacable reality, Kramer did not seem to realize fully the dangers of his situation. The same trust that had kept him from assessing the extent of the city's deterioration now kept him from understanding that his opponents would go to any lengths to defeat him. But he would not attempt to fight them in the same measure. Many of his own supporters were upset, for example, by the "political deadwood" that still remained at City Hall, they had expected him at least to attempt to fire some of these people, but he had not done so. Instead, the mayor glossed over everything with larger doses of hard work and concern. A priest who worked closely with Kramer on community problems remembers one event that, for him, symbolized Kramer's misjudgment. The Public Works' Department declared a strike during a bad snow storm. In response, Kramer and his top aides decided to clear the streets themselves. The administration actually spent an enjoyable day, driving snowplows and receiving enthusiastic compliments from citizens. Most important in their own view, they had "shown Graves" that nothing could keep them from serving and running the city. "It made you almost want to laugh if you weren't crying already," the priest recalls, "to see them on top of those snowplows and thinking they could defeat Graves and his crew that way. They thought they could change everything just by plowing over it. It was tragic. You wanted them to succeed so much, but, at the same time, you wanted to warn them it wouldn't work."

Kramer was, however, to learn his lesson—in two parts: in trying to build the city through urban renewal and in the destruction of the city through a riot.

Two days after he took office, Kramer was leafing through the papers Graves had left behind when he discovered a letter from the Department of Housing and Urban Development. It stated that HUD would not approve the city's "workable program" (a general statement of the year's development plans) and intended to halt all federal aid to the city. Graves had not bothered to inform Kramer of the immediate need for a workable new program. The new administration formulated an approved plan, which HUD praised as strikingly superior to Paterson's previous plans. However, Kramer's former rival John Wegner still headed the Housing Authority and would for another four years. Wegner proceeded to block so many of Kramer's renewal efforts that all urban renewal in Paterson was effectively halted.

The Housing Authority seemed not to recognize the change in administration. Kramer first named Mrs. Florence

Brawer to a vacancy on the Housing Authority where she
served as a frustrated and often amusing critic but was
consistently the one dissenting vote in matters of policy. Her
fellow commissioners continued to fill the paid staff with
machine friends who had little experience in building or
renewal. "G.I." Jimmy Vasile, one of the Grossi chauffeurs,
for example, was taken on as a relocation assistant. One day
he was directing the demolition crews and tore down two
wrong buildings before he was stopped. Kramer had long
wanted to establish a separate agency for renewal and leave
the Housing Authority with power only over building housing projects and related matters. In response to the continu-
ous succession of foul-ups such as Vasile's, the city Finance
Board (including two of Graves' appointees) unanimously
approved the mayor's request to revoke the Housing Authority's control of urban renewal. Wegner and two of his
commissioners went to court in protest and won the case.
When Kramer sought assistance from HUD, the federal
agency declined to intervene in what it called "a local dispute"; HUD merely cut off all money for Paterson until the
matter was straightened out.

After regaining control of renewal, Wegner's next move
was to rehire Bernard Lembo, the son of a fellow Housing
Authority commissioner, as director of planning and development. The federal government had informed Lembo five
times previously that the job had been phased out and could
not be paid for with federal money. The state Civil Service
Commission then claimed that Lembo possessed a resid-
ual right to employment with the Housing Authority and
"ordered" the authority to give him a post as a building
inspector, in spite of the fact that Lembo had failed the Civil
Service test for building inspectors. His failure wasn't generally known until Mrs. Brawer forced the matter into the
open. With a former chauffeur directing demolition and a

man who had not passed a building inspector's test as director of planning and development, the morass surrounding urban renewal in Paterson was providing a clue to the failure of urban renewal across the country. Paterson did not have renewal; it had $32 million of patronage and muscle.

Kramer did not comment publicly on these episodes. Hoping to regain federal funds (which had been cut off for seven months) by hiring a professional administrator, he first needed Wegner's approval. Wegner agreed to the professional administrator and, when federal funds were restored, released $75,000 to a construction firm under circumstances federal auditors described as "improper." A year and a half after Kramer took office he finally faced the fact that hard work alone would not bring about a change in urban renewal. The mayor had shrunk from the explosive issue of retaliating against his former election opponent, but, by now, he was left with little choice except to remove Wegner.

But the question was how. The authority had deposited $5.5 million in a noninterest-bearing account at a bank where Wegner was a stockholder and sat on the board of directors. His failure to state publicly his association with the bank constituted a minor violation of state law. Also, the authority had paid several thousand dollars for work for which there were no invoices or receipts, but suddenly the receipts appeared. Kramer finally settled on charges of inefficiency and neglect against Wegner and two other commissioners. These were civil charges, not criminal charges, and carried no penalty except the commissioners' removal from office. The case set a precedent as the first instance in the United States where unsalaried public-service commissioners appealed their ouster from office. The civil proceeding was cumbersome and time-consuming; since Paterson's charter did not provide for any real governing body or city council to take care of such matters, it was decided that the Finance Board should first hear the charges. Wegner and the others fought for months before the Finance Board, then appealed the case to Superior Court and finally brought it to the state Appellate Court. Why had they undertaken this enormous expense and trouble to retain unpaid posts? Graves adamantly denied having any influence on the proceedings. "I don't know what the hell they're doing," he commented. "If you ask me, the whole thing's idiotic."

The Finance Board's hearing of the charges, held in the dreary institutional green Aldermanic Chambers on the third floor of City Hall, quickly turned into a circus of vindictiveness. Spectators shouted invectives and opinions from the floor. Sam Raff, the commissioners' pudgy, fist-flailing lawyer, sometimes spoke for several hours at a stretch, dealing forth tirades that had little bearing on the charges at hand. "I want to remain alive. I don't want to be stuffed into your oppression, suppression, and repression!" he shouted pointedly at the Finance Board chairman who was an undertaker in his private business. City Counsel Joe Conn, normally unrufflable, presented the city's charges while steadily chewing on Life Savers to calm himself during the outbursts directed at him. "What a stinking bum you are," Harold Brown, one of the accused commissioners, told him. At other times Brown accused Conn, a reform Jew, of being Hitler and the elderly Finance Board commissioners of constituting "a lynch mob."

The commissioners, of course, retained their posts while they were on trial and, during this time, they were not idle. Within a ten-day period they did the following: First, they assigned Donald Raff, son of their defense attorney, the $5,500 part-time job of urban-renewal counsel and, on the basis of a New Jersey Civil Service law forbidding war veterans to be removed from public jobs, said he held the job as a lifetime post. Raff had served in the Reserves and was ineligible for this protection. However, his unit had been activated during the Berlin crisis and even though he spent the entire time stationed at Fort Knox, the authority declared him a war veteran. "It makes us look nuts," commented Mrs. Brawer. Next, Wegner delayed a long-planned middle-income housing project being sponsored by the United Automobile Workers Union. Wegner, who had previously favored the project, said he was no longer in favor of it since Kramer wanted it, and he did not intend to aid Kramer. That the city was desperate for all housing, particularly middle-income housing, did not seem to interest him. Last, Wegner read a thirty-second resolution stripping the professional administrator of power. The salaries for the urban-renewal staff, now without authority to carry out their jobs, added to the city's legal expenses for the duration of the hearings, costing thousands of dollars a month.

In the end, the Finance Board found the three commissioners guilty as charged of inefficiency and neglect and dismissed them from office; however, it was not until two years after Kramer had taken office that all the decisions were upheld and the mayor, smiling, stated. "I really feel as though I'm mayor of Paterson for the first time." Those two years were lost forever in a city which had no time to lose.

For many of the participants in these events, governing Paterson meant patronage and privileges, and they understood little about the city aside from these central struggles for power. But these events did not occur in a vacuum. They took place in a city where thirty-seven percent of the housing units were substandard, where tuberculosis and venereal disease were rampant, where unemployment was twice the national rate, and where hope was perhaps the last, slight factor holding the place together. To most people in Paterson—living in the Victorian mansions carved into tenements, floundering in a vague world bounded by self-doubt and suspicion—the names John Wegner, Tony Grossi, Ralph Ventrella, or "G.I." Jimmy Vasile meant nothing, but the actions of these men decided much. The stalled urban-renewal hearings, the shouting and soliloquies were a ludicrous side-show to reality. Kramer now began to feel almost physically sickened by the confines of the City Hall, where his careful, bright plans rotted. Two floors below him Ventrella continued to reject demolition orders; two floors above him the urban-renewal hearings droned on. Across the street Frank Graves sat and watched and, having made his point, moved his headquarters to Main Street. Kramer's time had run out.

Under optimum conditions the coalition that had brought Kramer to office could not have lasted. It was a coalition that, with its promise to "get this city back," had rallied the support of everyone from Wallacites to Black Panthers. It was a coalition that had unanimously agreed it wanted "good" and "honest" government, but there was no common definition of these terms. Did "good" government mean relentless law enforcement and full support for the police or a new appreciation for civil rights? Did "honest" government mean throwing out all the machine holdovers or working with them in hope of using their power for the city's benefit? Whatever the answers to such questions, many people in Paterson began to feel that Kramer had accomplished little in the way of substantial improvement. It is debatable whether some of his stalled programs, particularly urban renewal, if they had moved forward would have produced marked benefits for the small property owners clutching their homes against confiscatory taxes or made any change in blighted areas of the city. Had the city felt the stirrings of progress—seen abandoned buildings removed or new construction proceeding—a sense of expectation would, at least, have blunted the bitter edge of the growing disappointment. Paterson was starting to lose the astounding but tenuous unity that had seen Kramer elected.

The renewed discontent centered on more than the slow progress of specific programs. Paterson had for six years watched Graves charm, cajole, or compel the city to fulfill his every whim. His mastery, of course, stemmed partly from his being able to obtain the cooperation of everyone he needed, from the governor down to the City Hall janitor, and there was great initial understanding for Kramer's occupying the much different position of a joker in a stacked deck. But Paterson, with its tough, frontier sensibility, had little patience for the mayor's apparent unwillingness to deal with his opponents—or the city—forcefully. In the face of so many obstacles to his programs, Kramer appeared to have lost, not precisely his will, but his depth of commitment to the city he was fighting for. The mayor who had once had the good human sense to rush to Graham Avenue and "dance those kids until they fell over" was benumbed in a maze of building codes. His efforts, energetic as they were, had stopped at the surface. He suspended attempts to reform the police at the first sign of opposition. The Housing Authority hearings represented his first serious step toward taking command. But Paterson simply did not live on the surface; it lived in a deeply emotional, contradictory world. Graves had understood this world instinctively; he had understood that, given the passions and complexities of the urban situation, raw power was sometimes a necessary ingredient—and he understood that, above all, a city such as Paterson could stand least of all to drift. In the directionless vacuum beneath Kramer's struggle to patch over the city's problems with new programs and new ideas, Paterson's old fears and conflicts started to boil out of control. Where Kramer had not taken hold, the city took matters into its own hands.

The blacks were the first to act. Perhaps the death of Martin Luther King had infused them with a sense of time running out, for, in May 1968, one month after the assassination, the local branch of his organization, the Southern Christian Leadership Conference, sponsored a sit-in at City Hall, marking Paterson's first civil-rights' demonstration. From all points of view, it turned out to be a fitful and unsatisfying affair. Because of the tight rein that had prevailed in the city, few responsible people of any color possessed experience in holding peaceful demonstrations or negotiating over issues, and city agencies, particularly the police, were unfamiliar with handling situations that had virtually become routine in many cities. The very fact of a sit-in had an inordinately sensational effect on a public unaccustomed to such sights. Taking their first steps into the new world of sit-ins, the blacks were disorganized and their demands, to the public eye, seemed vague and contradictory. Their chief demand, for example, was that the police department be forbidden to use Mace for crowd control since it could cause eye damage. This hardly seemed the major issue among the several thousand legitimate complaints that Paterson's minority population could have made.

The demonstration caught Kramer off guard. He found it unjust that the very qualities he had tried to foster in the city—openness, free expression, an end to fear—should now be turned against him. Unsure of what to do, he neither negotiated with the demonstrators nor attempted to get them to leave the building. The sit-in, therefore, developed into a four-day sleep-in at City Hall, a spectacle that outraged public opinion. "It was awful," commented one woman who worked at City Hall and supported Kramer in other matters. "Every day we had to climb over all those bodies just to get to work."

Kramer probably became the only mayor in the United States to permit demonstrators to sleep in his City Hall, but in doing so, he set emotions on a collision course. He did not understand the insistent mood of the blacks, who, unimpressed by the mayor's "letting" them stay, accused him of "turning on the people who elected him," as one said, for his refusal to meet with them. The demonstrators were determined not to move without either the satisfaction of a meeting or the gratification of being dragged out. Nor did the mayor understand the fury of the whites at seeing City Hall literally "taken over." Kramer had put his faith in reason and, trying to avoid a confrontation, assumed that the blacks were bound to leave eventually. The fourth night of the sleep-in, the mayor met with Police Commissioner Edwin Englehardt. Kramer had decided to urge the demonstrators to leave by removing the cots they had brought and asked Englehardt to have this done by 6:00 A.M. the next morning. When Kramer arrived at City Hall the following day, he found the blacks gone, eight people arrested, and himself bombarded with brutality charges. The police said the arrests were necessary because the demonstrators hadn't given up the cots, but, in the conflicting accounts, it was not clear whether or not the police had warned the demonstrators before making arrests. One fact was clear, however; Kramer's order had specifically stated that the demonstrators be allowed to stay.

Kramer was shocked. The shrill attacks from all sides overwhelmed him. He seemed like a man moving through a bad dream, hoping for nothing better than to wake up before the end. The unnecessary bruises displayed by some of the demonstrators gave them a certain moral authority. He agreed to discuss everything, saying he would resign from office if it would ease the situation, and ultimately banned Mace. To his later regret, he also promised to fire the policemen accused of brutality if formal charges were filed against them. More than once he cautioned the people milling around his desk,

"Just don't hold a gun over the head of the mayor of Paterson." He spoke figuratively; no one had a gun. But it was a strange statement. Kramer had lost his authority.

As some of the participants later conceded, Paterson's first civil-rights skirmish—which ended when the mayor declined to meet again with the demonstration's leader and who, in turn, stood on the steps of City Hall and announced that he therefore refused to meet with the mayor—was more a comedy of errors than anything else. Yet, in the city's mood, it was taken in dead seriousness. That a few dozen blacks, supported by some clergymen, had paralyzed the mayor was a bad sign; that the police had publicly ignored orders was a dangerous one. Paterson was left with the feeling that the mayor could not control the city and with a reinforced fatalism. It began to seem that the city could no more obtain human renewal than it could urban renewal. As it turned out, the City Hall sleep-in was only a preview. In this atmosphere, seething, bitter, and unrestrained, Paterson fell apart.

A month and a half later, the mayor committed a serious error. On Sunday, June 31, 1968, the Puerto Ricans held their annual parade. A long hot spell, the tension following the sit-in, and the national gloom over war and assassination had combined to put the city in an ugly and restless mood. The Spanish leaders felt it was essential that Kramer review the parade. He never appeared; later he claimed he had been detained by an automobile breakdown. Graves helpfully pointed out that Kramer had a police radio in his car and could have summoned assistance. In any event, the fact remained that the mayor—who had also missed the Veteran's Day parade and consequently been denounced from flagpole to flagpole—had not grasped the city's insistence on having certain forms met and its pride bolstered. And pride was at a particularly low ebb among the Puerto Ricans, who not only felt excluded by language and culture, but, as the most recent arrivals, were at the bottom of everyone's list from the politicians to the dispensers of poverty programs. A friendly priest had sent Kramer an urgent, last-minute warning: "Domingo la fiesta o lunes el funeral" ("Sunday the fiesta or Monday the funeral"). The "funeral" started promptly Monday evening when a Puerto Rican opening a fire hydrant was arrested by a policeman, with thirty-two stitches' worth of force, and the excited crowd that had viewed the arrest marched down to headquarters in protest.

It is doubtful that the mayor's attending the parade would have prevented the ensuing riot, but Kramer had left himself open to significant reproaches from both sides. Conservatives charged that his "soft" stand during the sit-in encouraged an atmosphere ripe for disorder; for the minorities, that the riot started when a Puerto Rican was brutally arrested proved their contention that Kramer might have started nice programs such as housing inspections and summer activities, but he had not seriously wrestled with the inequities of city government. Interestingly enough, the disillusion of both sides settled on the same issue—Mayor Kramer had not taken charge of Paterson.

The Spanish section of Main Street cooled with minimal damage following three days of rioting. Both rioters and police sustained some injuries, but no casualties; and the State Police, when called, did not consider the disturbance serious enough to warrant their attention. A few weeks later only the boards nailed over broken windows remained as mementos to the hot nights filled with police sirens and sullen crowds. But something had happened in Paterson that no boards would ever cover over. In the early-morning hours of July 3, halfway through his term, Kramer encountered the final realization of what it meant to be mayor of Paterson.

In the early morning on July 3 a group of policemen

held a secret rendezvous. They had chosen a grimly appropriate location—in front of the Washington Casket Company along a deserted section of Ward Street. After their meeting, the patrolmen invaded the Fourth Ward, striking specifically against their known critics and incidentally against any black person in their path. They first assaulted the S.C.L.C. headquarters, smashing the windows and throwing tear-gas bombs inside; then they rampaged down Graham Avenue, the commercial area of the Fourth Ward, wrecking black-owned stores, leaving victims beaten senseless behind on the streets. The attack lacked even the excuse of being a spontaneous outburst taken in the midst of a riot; the riot in the Spanish section on the other side of town, which the rest of the force was working to quell, in fact, served as a convenient cover.

This premeditated attack absolutely and completely trapped Kramer. In his worst imaginings of what twists the city's life might take, he had not conceived that it would be some members of the police department who would brutally violate their public trust and risk setting the entire city in flames. Moreover, since the attack could not easily be dismissed as the action of a few renegade policemen, its dimensions were appalling. A later grand jury investigation headed by the state attorney general's office, although concluding that it was unable to pinpoint criminal responsibility for the raid, did vote on fifty-nine possible indictments involving twenty-six policemen. A presentment issued after a county grand jury investigation asked why superior officers had not known the location of the units involved in this "unlawful and shocking action." The grand jury said it was "feasible" that the raid had occurred without a comand officer's necessarily being aware but that other testimony cast doubt upon the "widespread professed ignorance." Although some city officials, civil-rights leaders, and other insiders later found out exactly how high in the department the plans for the raid had gone, the public in general never knew. No one in a position of responsibility in Paterson could face the consequences of openly admitting such failure in leadership. As for the mayor, the dimensions of what had happened seemed to have overwhelmed him. In the wake of the recent riot, conservative public opinion would not tolerate action taken against the police. Kramer rejected insistent requests for a personal probe or convening the Police and Fire Board to start an investigation and, instead, he sidestepped the issue by calling in the F.B.I. to handle it.

The mayor was accused of allowing a terrible injustice to go unpunished solely to protect himself politically. There was truth to this charge, but there was a deeper reason for his reaction. Kramer had learned about the attack from an early-morning phone call to his home. "I felt physically and emotionally sickened when I put down the receiver," he recalled much later. "Of course, it was Nazi Germany. What else is there to say?" Kramer had wanted to rebuild Paterson, to present "practical solutions," to give the city "real things for its benefit." Stalling renewal, blocking a judge, and the other harassments might be expected, but this playing with life and death made him recoil; it was an uncompromising reality that was altogether outside his experience.

A reporter recalls seeing Kramer at police headquarters that night. "He seemed to be completely shaken. Then two policemen came in with a prisoner and I remember it very well because it struck me that there was something strange about the prisoner. He was wearing a white tee shirt and he had a large gash on his forehead. The blood had just started to show. I remember thinking that if the police had had any cause to hit him while they were arresting him, the blood would have flowed to his tee shirt by this time. It was still spotless. Obviously they had stopped just outside the door to have a go at him. They walked by Kramer and he saw it

and sort of shuddered. Of course, he was wrong, but you had
to feel sorry for him."

Halfway through his term Kramer presided over a city
which had turned from a place where he proudly walked the
streets to one scarred by flames and bitterness, where he could
barely find a supporter. Half the city held him if not personally responsible for the riot, then responsible for letting the
city run wild. The other half felt he had broken his promise
to bring honesty and justice to Paterson. For the blacks,
particularly, their worst fears of being innocently cut down
in the streets had come true. The mayor took little action and
called this descent into chaos "a bad Goosey Night."

Was it his fault? He had tried to live by his promises,
to carry out the "white papers" released during the campaign,
to trust the city and treat it with fairness, and found defeat
at every turn. If this was the reality, if others could tear down
what he was trying to build, if he could not reach the Paterson
that lay beneath the layers of filth and callousness, then this
was not the city he had won and hoped to serve. The mental
images from his first two years as mayor must have been
inescapable: the inauguration in top hats, dancing kids
"until they fell over," hands reaching out for his on walking
tours, and finally that night, the dimly lit police station, the
blood. Wherever the blame lay, nothing could change the
fact that running Paterson was his responsibility.

The rumors that Kramer intended to quit grew stronger.
Frank X. Graves was among those most interested, but the
idea did not please him. Graves was not a man who liked to
win by default and he was waiting for the public triumph of
the next election. "I hope he doesn't do that," commented
the former mayor. "He's doing so bad, he's the best weapon
I've got."

They [Americans] had inherited a system of law fashioned for the needs of a small, rural society and designed to safeguard the rights of property rather than persons; could they adapt that law to an urbanized and democratic society which placed human above property rights?

—HENRY STEELE COMMAGER
The American Mind *

The melancholy drama of expectation, disappointment, and recrimination enacted in Paterson has been witnessed in many other American cities. Certainly both Mayor Kramer and the citizens of Paterson tended to view their failure in conventional terms: either Kramer was just another "politician" of false promise or Paterson was just another city "impossible to govern." Yet neither response is satisfactory. Kramer's election had been only one of several urban-reform elections across the country in the late 1960s. The triumphs of dedicated liberals in traditionally machine-

* Copyright 1950 by Yale University Press. Reprinted by permission of Yale University Press.

121 ☐ ☐ ☐

run cities, together with a growing national awareness of the cities' ills, newly designated federal funds, and burgeoning urban programs, held out a momentary hope, which, with few exceptions, has gone unrealized. How can so many cities go through the difficult process of putting a "good" administration into office and find that so little has changed? How could Kramer, like many other "dynamic, young mayors," find himself so frustrated and powerless?

On the whole, American cities probably had more technically honest governments during the late 1960s than at any other period within the past century. The cities certainly had more public money than ever before in their history, but neither the millions of dollars nor the mayoral styles, ranging from Lindsay to Daley, have made much visible impact. Political change and surface reform within the current urban structure have failed as consistently as money poured into that structure has been wasted. It is important, therefore, to look at the premises underlying American urban life and the haphazard, antidemocratic, and often brutal systems of government to which the cities in this country are bound. Paterson and other cities are not only fighting against political machines, terrifying crime waves, housing crises, and other signs of decay; they are fighting against an American tradition of refusal to value the cities as equals; they have always been, and still are, divorced from the mainstream of American life.

Although the cities now constitute nearly a majority of the American population, their inferior status in the American political structure has not changed. As Constance Green commented in *The Rise of Urban America:*

The problems of urban America, in short, had become national problems. Yet, the political philosophy of the United States still regarded them in the category of local affairs. The creation of a federal Department of Urban Affairs comparable to the Department of Agriculture, a proposal first tendered early in the century in Theodore Roosevelt's day, received little serious attention. Whereas the 1962 budget for the Department of Agriculture ran to some $7.4 billion, the sum allotted to urban problems totalled about $400 million, much of it "authorized," but not appropriated. . . . The American people recognized the well-being of the farm as a national concern. They were not yet seeing the city in a similar light.*

The political philosophy of the United States does not seriously recognize the cities for good reason. Every level of government presumes the cities' impotence: the congressional seniority system that protects rural committee heads; the states, which are turning from a previously rural bias to serve "the new majority" in the suburbs; the counties, those obscure governing units whose very obscurity consistently enables them to build an exacting power and patronage base for manipulating the cities within their borders. In turn, the paralysis of such a large segment of the population enables these other interest groups to retain their power. In a nation where everyone can vote, it provides a built-in brake against the possibility of real democracy; it is the safeguard of corporate despotism and the guardian of corruption. Dealing with the cities, in short, involves ominous questions of rights and powers. Rather than face the implications of meeting the cities' legitimate demands, the United States has chosen to leave urban residents disenfranchised to the point where their position might best be described as feudal.

Like many cities in the 1960s, Paterson found it had to some extent graduated from machine government, but graduated to what? Although the city had taken the first step toward controlling its own affairs, its most critical needs—

housing, transportation, law enforcement, social and political organization, even its moral standards (the anti-gambling and blue laws, which are favorites of state legislatures)—still depended on the whims of outside forces.

In Paterson there is a man named Julius Threet, a successful real-estate agent and local developer. Mr. Threet is a man of vision. "Look at this," he says, pointing out the expanse of Paterson. "A city like this, built on hills and with the river running through. It should be beautiful." Mr. Threet also has a slogan: "Pride Through Ownership." Having both a vision and a slogan has made him more determined than other men. He decided to renovate some of Paterson's worst tenements, turning them into nonprofit cooperative apartments. In 1968 he obtained a Federal Housing Administration mortgage for this purpose. On paper it looked like any one of the some eleven million mortgages, all but a handful of them for suburban homes, that the F.H.A. has guaranteed since it was established in 1934. It was, in fact, an extraordinary mortgage. As far as Threet has been able to determine, it marked the first time that the F.H.A. had guaranteed a private mortgage in any ghetto area of New Jersey. This means that for the four decades since the F.H.A. came into existence and started setting national mortgage policies, the federal government has, in effect, forbidden individual, private ownership of homes in the inner cities and left them with little choice for housing other than public housing, housing owned by slumlords, and the type of people who can procure loan-shark financing outside legal commercial channels. It had, moreover, taken Threet three years of cutting through the F.H.A.'s red tape to obtain the mortgage.

It hardly seems possible that, in a nation whose founding was largely based on the principle that men should be free in the enjoyment of their own property and whose growth largely rested on its being able to offer homesteads to people who would have remained landless in their own countries, the very government agency established to promote home-building and ownership should cut off vast urban areas from the means to participate in what is virtually regarded as an American right. Yet this reversal of values is the consistent theme of Washington's relations with the cities. The record is not just one of neglect in monetary terms. It is a neglect that is much more profound and crippling. Washington has refused to confront the cities within the terms of its responsi-bilities under the federal system. As Henry Commager has noted, the American legal system was formulated for a rural society and to protect property rights. Until the law recognizes urban rights as a whole and the protections that urban individuals require, then it seems doubtful that the cities will be able to function as an integral part of American society no matter how much money and how many programs they are granted.

Some recent Supreme Court decisions reveal the extent to which the cities are outcasts. The cities themselves did not receive equal rights until the "one-man, one-vote" decision of 1962. That the cities have been gerrymandered out of equable political representation for nearly the entire lifetime of the United States is a profound comment on the premises of American democracy and has created an imbalance of government that it will take decades to erase. For the manage-ment of their immediate surroundings, tenant rights are the most crucial commodity urban residents can possess. Yet in 1972, in what tenant advocates had hoped would be a land-mark decision, the Supreme Court ruled that tenants have no constitutional guarantee to a "warranty of hability"; that is to say, it ruled that tenants do not have the right to withhold rent even while their landlords are in court for alleged violations of housing laws or failures to provide minimal maintenance services. The court said that a tenant's duty to pay his rent and a landlord's duty to obey the law were separate matters, and it was not a denial of due process to force one party to fulfill his end of the contract and not the other. In the suburbs such matters are quite simple; if a man pays his fuel bill, he gets heat. In the cities a man pays no matter what.

The court followed up this decision with one, in 1973, that was one of the most astonishing rulings in its history; it said, in effect, that urban children have no constitutional guarantee to equal education. The case involved a challenge to the states' financing public education primarily from the property taxes raised in local districts. Under this system of financing, it is impossible for poorer localities, particularly the cities, to provide the money for equal education even though urban residents pay much higher property taxes and proportionately devote a larger percentage of their income to the support of the schools than do suburbanites. According to the court, the Constitution did not explicitly mention education as a protected right; therefore, an American child, living one foot over a man-made boundary line, can be handicapped for life by bad schools. Moreover, this decision forces the cities to continue levying the high property taxes that are pushing out their middle-class.* The court's position is especially unfathomable since it had already declared that educational equality between the races is a constitutional imperative. Do not urban children live under

* It is not the position of this author that justice requires entirely equalizing taxation. Cities, in general, provide more facilities—public colleges, cultural events, just to name two—for their residents and, of course, should pay for those things. The very congestion of urban life that provides the attraction and excitement for those people who live in the cities by choice rather than by segregation makes municipal services more expensive. However, there are basic services, such as education and transportation, that are simply necessary for society to function and to which people are entitled with equal access.

the same Constitution? The closeness of the decision, 5 to 4, indicates that they may not now, but perhaps will be permitted to do so some time in the future.

In addition to the prima facie failure of the law to recognize urban rights, federal agencies have not made a concerted effort to enforce existing laws (particularly in the areas of political and corporate corruption) that are essential to the cities' ability to maintain legitimate control over their affairs. Paterson's record in this regard is striking. In the city's entire history the federal government has taken only two actions aimed at protecting the basic rights of its citizens. In 1969 and again in 1970 federal grand juries indicted several policemen on civil-rights charges. In both cases, the charges were dismissed in court. The New Jersey division of the U.S. attorney's office seems not to have noticed that it is located in one of the most corrupt states in the nation. While machine politicians threatened voters and squandered public resources, it scarcely protested until 1970, when it was taken over by crusading attorneys and dozens of local officials were indicted and convicted.

Congress, in recent decades, has added its own measure of mischief by working actively to reinforce the imbalance between the cities and the rest of the country. In 1965, after soundly defeating the proposal twice in the early 1960s, Congress, which had been annually expending eighteen times more money for farm programs than for the cities, at last consented to establish the Department of Housing and Urban Development as a cabinet post. The cities were not only elevated to a status equaling that of the Post Office, but the subsequent proliferation of urban programs gave the impression that they were finally receiving their due. But despite the publicity surrounding urban aid, urban residents still did not have access to the most significant forms of federal largesse. It is symbolic that aid to the cities should have been considered so special, when Washington has been steadily underwriting the farms and lavishing subsidies on the suburbs. Two domestic programs in particular stand out in terms of the billions poured into them and the changes they have wrought in the nation. The National Highway Act and F.H.A. mortgages have not just benefited the suburbs, but have benefited them at the direct expense of the cities.

The National Highway Act could well be described as a unique method of accounting under which the cities get to pay for their own demise. Highways encourage the movement of both industry and the middle class to the suburbs, but the cities have to tear down their own housing, creating social havoc, to make room for more access routes. Urban drivers, too, pay the gasoline taxes which pay for the highways, but since these taxes can only be used for interstate roads, and not for local purposes, their money supports the convenience of suburbanites while encouraging a form of transportation that is economically disastrous for the cities. Paterson once had four railroads connecting it to its markets; the federal government made no effort to save them, and the city now has one railroad, which does not even reach New York. The Port of New York, the access to the national and international marketplace, is only a few tantalizing miles in the distance, but the city is literally severed from its economic potential. Even with Route 80's completion, without mass transportation, Paterson will be unable to manage either the truck congestion for industry or the commuter traffic for offices; and it will continue to lose out to suburban industrial parks conveniently bordering superhighways.

If transportation policy has been weighted against the cities' competing commercially, federal housing policy has been loaded against their surviving socially. Before the establishment of the F.H.A., the accompanying creation of a national mortgage market, and the development of a large, institutionalized banking system, urban residents had relatively equal access to mortgages through small neighborhood banks, which were interested in their surrounding communities and which have now largely disappeared. Then, in the 1930s the newly created F.H.A. for the first time set national mortgage policies and, as it declined to guarantee mortgages in urban areas, commercial banks quite naturally followed suit by declining to make loans in these same areas. The F.H.A.'s policy was not rooted in malice, but in two traditional American values—a predilection for new things and a mistrust of the cities. Nevertheless, its effects were malicious. As Jane Jacobs noted in the *Death and Life of Great American Cities,* the resulting rush to the suburbs and spread of urban slums did not "come about by accident—and still less by the myth of free choice between the cities and the suburbs." During the Depression and World War II little new housing was constructed. It was natural, as people became financially able to improve their living conditions, for them to do so. Those who desired to remain in the cities could not obtain mortgages either for renovation or for new construction and were pushed to the suburbs, leaving behind neighborhoods that could only be abandoned or taken over by slumlords.

It is not only through mortgages that federal policies favor suburban housing. Homeowners are permitted to deduct mortgage interest and real-estate taxes from their income tax; apartment dwellers, even though their rents reflect these costs, are not. These tax deductions, which are nothing more than individual subsidies, not only amount to billions in "welfare" for the suburbs annually, but greatly surpass the money that the federal government spends each year on housing programs for the poor:

In 1962, the federal government spent an estimated $820 million to subsidize housing for poor people. (The sum includes public housing, public assistance, and savings because of income tax deductions.) In the same year, the federal government spent an estimated $2.9 billion to subsidize those with middle-incomes or more. (The sum includes only savings from income tax deductions.) That is, the federal government spent three and a half times as much for those who were not poor as for those who were.*

Although public housing construction has increased since this intensive study was made, there has also been such a large movement to the suburbs that these inconsistencies in underwriting housing probably have not changed significantly.

Even without this favoritism, there would have been some movement to the suburbs. The space requirements of modern industry often necessitate leaving urban areas. Just as there are many people who would prefer to live in the cities if conditions were improved, there are many people who prefer to live in the suburbs under any conditions but the changeover occurred at a breakneck speed which could not be absorbed by even the best-organized community. Between 1960 and 1970 Paterson experienced a population turnover of forty-four percent based on racial characteristics alone, which means its true turnover was much higher. The consequences of creating such a large number of rootless people—the crime, violence, family and social dissolution—have been fairly consistent throughout the world and certainly have been proven over and over again in America—from the Western frontier to the cities to, most recently and most ironically, the hastily contrived suburbs.

By the 1960s the cities had decayed to such a degree that

* Alvin Schorr, *Social Service Review*, cited in *The States and the Urban Crisis*, American Assembly Series (Englewood Cliffs, N.J.: Prentice-Hall).

it was impossible to continue ignoring them and a unique moment in American history arrived—the first national consensus that "something had to be done" about the cities and the first willingness to grant to them a measure of attention and financial consideration. It was a moment that was largely wasted. Urban aid was designed neither to promote the independence of the cities nor to equalize their status but was presented pretty much in the manner of foreign aid, framed to keep the "dangerous" cities uniquely controlled and regulated. In the end it was precisely at the moment when the United States decided to help its cities that the destructiveness of its urban attitudes became most clear.

In *Democracy in America* Alexis de Tocqueville discussed the unique tasks that municipalities of independence and integrity perform in a democratic society. They are a bulwark against the potential tyranny of the central authority, whose natural aim is steadily to draw more powers into its own hands. Local institutions provide an immediate outlet for the political and social passions which might otherwise have to be put down forcibly by the central government. In a setting where officials are elected by their neighbors (rather than appointed by a distant central authority), the designs of the ambitious are kept in check. Interests may differ from locality to locality, but where people are left with enough power to administer their immediate affairs to their satisfaction, their differences have less chance of becoming points of contention. The practice of solving problems locally guarantees vitality of government and attaches citizens to the interests of their nation, an attachment that in a dictatorship can only be assured by force. De Tocqueville, greatly impressed by the town meetings of New England, thought the high degree of municipal independence in the United States, as compared to centralized administration in Europe, constituted a real point of genius in the American political system. "Municipal institutions," he concluded, "constitute the strength of free nations. Town meetings are to liberty what primary schools are to science; they bring it within people's reach, they teach men how to use and enjoy it."

The havoc that mass federal intervention caused in the cities can almost entirely be blamed on violating the integrity of the cities. Certainly the cities received money, but since they had little choice in how this money was spent, it served to underwrite the federal view of the cities, not to deal with the realities of urban life. Education, housing, transportation, garbage collection, freedom to vote without fear, and other basics received little attention. In Paterson, the new federal largesse instead provided such things as a Teenage Charm Center, a Neighborhood Youth Corps Center with a closed-circuit TV system, free movies, an occasional rat roundup, and a $100,000 unemployment survey that was never completed because no one got around to feeding the data into the computer. It is interesting to compare these items to the actual problems that real people who live in Paterson most often cite for their disaffection: high taxes, bad schools, and crime. By 1970 the city was receiving a mere $38,400 annually in federal aid to education, one small grant for its police department to start the community relations program, and not a penny in the kind of direct aid or revenue sharing that could be used to lower taxes.

In addition, the cities were not considered as a whole, but as if they contained two separate parts—a downtown business district and a surrounding ring of the criminal, the poor, and the aged. Like many cities, Paterson received the bulk of its federal aid, some $38 million in the decade between 1960 and 1970, for urban renewal. Urban renewal consists of clearing tracts of land which are then theoretically sold to developers for the purpose of erecting office buildings, factories, stores, and other supposed assets to the city. Renewal is the most socially destructive and financially wasteful program that has been foisted on the cities. The reasoning behind it seems to be rooted in the stringent concept that the cities' primary goal is a material splendor that should be pursued at any cost, even if it means sacrificing the city itself. Renewal initially produces more harmful effects than a phalanx of offices and factories could possibly offset. It destroys structurally sound low-cost housing and rips through neighborhoods and, by doing so, it creates yet another source of social disorder where rootlessness and disorder are already killing problems. It exacts an incalculable cost to the "well-being of the individual citizen" in demolishing the fabric of his life. The helpless rage that people experience as a result of being pushed out by the government is something from which many of them never quite recover; a decade after Bunker Hill was started, former residents of that area still talked bitterly about being "robbed" of their homes.

It is poetic justice, but something the cities can hardly afford, that the business aspect of urban renewal customarily fails, too. Most cities have experienced tremendous difficulty in attracting developers for their cleared land. If other conditions are not favorable—such as a reasonable tax rate, good transportation, and a viable surrounding community—developers will not invest in an area no matter how much money has been spent renewing it. Yet, even though Paterson had not been able to complete Bunker Hill after a decade of trying to entice developers to that project, the federal government extended the city another $32 million to start demolishing its downtown in similar fashion.

It would be hard to find one person in Paterson who would describe the city's major problem as a dearth of office buildings. Had the citizens of Paterson been given an outright choice in the use of this money, it is unlikely that they would have spent it on the endless exercise in bulldozing. They would have used it, quite naturally, for their own self-interest and, in so doing, would have funneled it to the basic, real problems of the city. Paterson's urban-renewal budget alone, not to mention other federal aid, could not only have equalized the city in relation to its suburbs, but markedly improved both its business and its social climate. These millions could have given the city a significantly lower tax rate, better schools, and could have enabled the city to clean up—improvements that would have provided many more attractions for investors than sterile acres of dirt sitting desolately in the middle of a slum.

The federal government, in general, represents the individual interests of a private-property system which is little aware that cities not only do but must function differently than suburbs. Suburbs are places of retreat whose residents prefer to live apart. The job of the cities, as Lewis Mumford has written, "is to provide the maximum number of favorable opportunities for large populations to intermingle and interact, to interchange their human facilities and aptitudes as well as their economic goods and services, to stimulate and intensify by frequent contact and collaboration many common interests that would otherwise languish." * The organized focal point that cities provide for creativity, inventiveness, communication, administration, in brief, for the interfusion of society is perhaps their most vital function. The federal approach—divide and "solve"—has consistently succeeded in destroying the cities' ability to carry out this function. Economic programs, such as urban renewal, were divorced from the cities' social fabric and the federal practice of holding out tidbits for competing interest groups has

---

* From *The Urban Prospect*. Copyright © 1956 by Lewis Mumford. Reprinted by permission of Harcourt Brace Jovanovich, Inc.

helped turn the cities into the warring factions they present today.

By presuming that the cities were composed of nothing except problems, this unrealistic approach drastically reinforced the nation's already destructive attitude toward its cities. Nothing was done to encourage the cities' assets, to help the middle class to stay, to preserve existing housing, to improve the basic services that are of equal concern to all citizens. "Paterson offers no reason for its best citizens to continue living here," one prominent critic pointed out. How could it? With its own resources so strained, almost anything it could do for its citizens depended upon the programs offered by the federal government and nothing in the federal approach presumed that "the best people" might want to stay in the cities. It is important, once again, to realize fully what these policies say about American urban attitudes. The programs of the 1960s were not conceived by ill-intentioned people, but by people who, for the most part, possessed a genuine concern for the cities. Yet the result of this decade of concentrated national attention to the cities was that they were still not places where normal people lived.

In the end the massive federal programs and their concentration on material goals at the expense of people placed the cities under a "supra-government" that functioned out of the reach of public consent and public influence. This government simply made up its own "laws" in the guise of procedures, guidelines, and regulations. Its officials were not elected by or answerable to the public. Paterson, then, to some extent, had graduated from machine government only to find itself in the throes of government by bureaucracy. There wasn't much difference; both had a vested interest in dependent cities. Machines protect themselves from the public through bribery and corruption and strengthen their hands by creating more and more "public" positions. In similar fashion bureaucracies protect themselves from the public through a quagmire of guidelines, Civil Service regulations, and other obstructions, while their growth, too, rests on their ability to increase their number of "clients." Cities now have to hire consultants for the single purpose of writing applications for federal money: a request for a Model Cities grant alone runs to nearly 200 pages. The insularity of these programs leaves them wide open to political manipulation from their general focus down to the smallest details. The Task Force, Paterson's O.E.O. program, has actually been subject to more demonstrations than City Hall—mainly on the part of the poor, who charged they were being "pushed out by politicians." On one occasion, washing machines installed in a senior citizens' housing project were filled with sponges bearing the message "Vote for Wegner."

Last, and most important, whatever tenuous grounding in integrity and independence that municipal governments had had previously was undermined by federal programs. It is difficult enough for urban residents to fight both the state and federal governments. But when municipal governments themselves are invested with the authority behind massive federal programs, the battle of urban residents to retain control over their own life choices becomes almost futile. The result is that there is no "natural process" of government. Everything is decided by one or another overriding level of government. The vitality and community spirit that no money or programs can buy is crushed; and the only contact that people affected by government decisions have with the process of government is in futilely venting their wrath and bitterness. Once an essential brake on "the designs of the ambitious" is removed, the raw power that these programs confer on officials spreads, infecting the city's schools, police, and other institutions. "Considering the kind of people a big-money program like urban renewal attracted and the influence they got in the city," states Mrs. Brawer, "I think one of the things that could have really saved Paterson was if urban renewal had been cut off years ago."

State governments, because they serve only the immediate majority that controls them, take an even more hostile attitude toward the cities than the federal government. Congressmen at least deal with national concerns and can be prevailed upon to consider the needs of areas outside their own constituencies. State legislators, on the other hand, myopically handle only the most local interests and prejudices. They see no focal points of cooperation, such as foreign relations and the economy. In the major urbanized states, the cities now make up about forty percent of the population, but, since suburban and rural interests possess the population advantage to beat out their urban competitors, the concentrated size of the cities often brings them no more consideration. State government, in short, represents nothing but the tyranny of a slim majority over the urban minority. The prescient de Tocqueville considered this one of the weakest features of the American system and felt that the structure of state government could well be a source of anarchy that "may be attributed to the omnipotence of the majority, which may at some future time urge the minorities * to desperation and oblige them to have recourse to physical force." Certainly that prediction has been borne out in New Jersey.

New Jersey is a state which, in the words of columnist John Fischer, is "totally uncalled-for." Like many states, its

---

* De Tocqueville was not referring to racial minorities, whose injustices were not a feature of local politics in 1835, but to minorities of interest, indicating again that the structural deficiencies which hamper the cities often work impartially.

boundaries do not reflect a "natural" governing area of population concentration, economic interdependence, or other mutual interests. The northern area looks toward New York as its capital; the southern part, to Philadelphia. The real state capital, Trenton, is neatly tucked away along the banks of the Delaware River. Recent investigations have revealed that corruption strangles every organ of state government, but corruption is hardly the only problem in New Jersey. Its government is not an administrative and lawmaking machine, but a collection of small medieval duchies, jealously guarded citadels of power. Sectionalism is the hallmark of most state governments, but New Jersey's particular geographical ambivalence, whereby it is divided in half, has created an especially virulent strain. Except to block conflict-of-interest legislation and vote themselves raises, the legislators usually decline to cooperate. Paterson and Passaic County, for example, are almost annually flooded. The Passaic River is not wide and would be inexpensive to control. The state geologist first recommended that it be dammed in 1888, but recent flood-control legislation was defeated by widespread opposition such as that from Essex County, which maintained that its crime problem was as devastating as the Passaic's floods. Meanwhile, the state has expended more on emergency flood relief than it would cost for elementary dredging of the river.

New Jersey, for various reasons, has also taken a particularly stern attitude toward its cities. It has no major city, such as New York, Chicago, or Los Angeles, to call attention to urban concerns. The state has an unusually high proportion of both new white residents and new black residents. The whites were generally people escaping the blacks in New York and the blacks were generally people escaping the whites in the South, and the two sets of refugees were hardly delighted to meet again. One group, however, was in the majority. Rural and suburban legislators in New Jersey see it as their duty to keep the "threatening" cities as weak as possible. This end is accomplished by many means: granting the cities weak charter rights that prevent them from making a move on their own, gerrymandering legislative districts, stacking tax and aid formulas against the cities. There is perhaps no state that so thoroughly drains its cities as does New Jersey. In 1969 the Republican chairman of the state legislative Committee on Urban Problems blasted the Republican-controlled legislature for actually concentrating state aid on wealthy communities. The results have been predictable. No other state presents the same spectacle of solid suburban wealth alongside urban squalor. There is no other state where five of the six largest cities have rioted and where riots have become a fact of life, not only in the larger cities, where they are "expected," but in smaller cities, with populations under 100,000.

New Jersey, aside from direct efforts to suppress the influence of the cities within the state, has also failed to recognize the protection and different requirements that urban governments need simply to operate efficiently inside their own boundaries. In Paterson in 1969, for example, one slumlord alone owed back taxes on 135 buildings, a situation that could be found in almost any major city. State law prevented the city from foreclosing on these buildings for two years, by which time the slumlord would probably have abandoned them anyway, meaning that other taxpayers would have had to make up the costs for educating the thousand or more children in those buildings as well as for bearing the expense of providing other city services. The law preventing foreclosure was meant to protect individual homeowners (in other words, suburbanites) in temporary financial straits from losing their homes; but by not distinguishing between private and commercial ownership, it permitted one man to relieve the city of more money legally than it probably lost through street crime in several months, in addition to encouraging the urban syndrome of slums and abandonment.

The question of how the cities can fight such practices is an extremely serious one. Even should they receive intelligently applied funds to deal with their real problems, their integrity will always be threatened as long as their basic organization and functions remain in the hands of suburban and rural legislators whose own concerns are directly opposed to urban interests. It was, of course, folly to have placed the cities in the minority position throughout all levels of government. It is also folly to expect that the states will voluntarily rectify this situation. In 1969, for example, New Jersey Governor Richard Hughes attempted to ameliorate the cities' position with a special urban aid package. Hughes treated some reluctant assemblymen to a tour of Newark. They declared themselves "appalled" by what they saw and voted $12 million, a little more than half of his original request, to be divided among the state's six largest cities. The share for each was hardly enough to build one grade school. One assemblyman had particularly remarked about his shock at seeing naked children playing in the streets of an American city.

For the cities, significant change from within the American federal system can only result from Washington's recognizing its responsibility to define their rights. As James Madison wrote in *The Federalist,* the responsibility of a republic is "not only to guard society against the oppression of its rulers, but to guard one part of the society against the injustice of the other part." This hope, however, may be a long time in being realized. In the recent decision on property taxes and the schools, for example, the Supreme Court recommended equal education as a goal for state legislatures, a goal which they have had two centuries to pursue. Among the many quirks of state aid formulas in New Jersey, the one urban officials cite most often and most bitterly is a provision whereby the state reimburses suburban and rural localities for seventy-five percent of their school bus costs, but only ten percent of the bill for inner-city children needing "special services." The practical effect of this provision is that children who live in pleasantly spaced communities and ride a bus receive sixty-five percent more help from the state than do ghetto children who are emotionally disturbed. The government of New Jersey is particularly weak in its administrative powers, unusually corrupt in practice, and notably backward in providing state services at all levels. Despite these idiosyncrasies, its urban posture is typical. The pattern of state aid's being concentrated outside the cities is repeated throughout the nation. A 1967 study of the thirty-six largest U.S. cities showed that, on the average, these cities received eighty-one percent less state aid to education than their surrounding suburbs.

In a sense, then, federal irresponsibility and state bias toward the cities is calculated. It is advantageous to government at all levels to have such a large proportion of the population paralyzed. The cities' weaknesses and the freedom that machines have had in keeping urban populations voiceless are the strong links in the chain of "special interests" that surround both the Congress and state legislatures. As a result, Paterson has been ruled by a regime that conventional political theory would say simply could not arise in a democracy.

In New Jersey the county government controls three critical functions: elections, welfare, and the court system (judges, juries, investigations, and arrests or lack of arrests). The counties' control of these services has given the machines a back door to controlling the cities through yet another layer of government whose obscurity is as advantageous as its functions are vital. In some respects the county is litle more than an excuse to underwrite political activity with public money.

It is this which gives the machines an extraordinary edge. Politics is notably time-consuming, and for most people it can be only a volunteer activity. The county, however, has 1,500 jobs to offer, putting people in a position to do favors. Its employment opportunities, added to its $35-million budget, give the county an enormous lever for patronage. On occasion, the Freeholders, or county commissioners, have been forced to admit that some county jobs are so useless (such as the $6,000 annual stipend for the part-time secretary to the county supervisor of roads) that they are not certain why the position exists or what work it is supposed to entail. As for the budget, there is no central administrator to account for the money. It is obvious where some of it goes. In 1968, for example, the Freeholders were planning to purchase a $1-million golf course while claiming that the county could not afford one drug treatment program. It is not, however, always so clear how the county disperses its funds.

These are mere details compared to the county's real powers. The Board of Elections is crucial to political battles, and the welfare department allows for some manipulation, but the county's trump card is its court system. The judges, the grand juries, the prosecutor's office, the detectives, and investigators may represent the administration of justice, but they also represent the final power, the final arbitrator—and the final threat. In New Jersey cities do not have their own district attorneys and are dependent on the county for the investigation and disposition of all but minor cases.

Nothing better illustrates the collapse of normal government functions in Passaic County than its administration of justice. Heading the county prosecutor's office was John Thevos, a rather genial, balding man, who kept quietly in the background while the county's warring factions ran free. Grossi had seen Thevos nominated for the positon, but he personally had not tried one case during his eleven years in office. In addition to heading a staff of assistant prosecutors, Thevos also had a staff of twenty-six detectives and investigators, all political appointees, who were supposed to investigate illegal activities in the county. Assignment Judge John Crane, the court administrator, was infuriated one day to find only one detective out of the entire staff at work in the office. Meanwhile, the rackets flourished; drugs poured into Paterson, and there seemed to be no time for the Prosecutor's Office to follow various suggestions, like one made by a Grand Jury investigating riot conditions, that it might probe the apparently protected position of slumlords.

Even in this indolent state, the prosecutor's office was in better condition than the courts themselves, which had almost ceased to function. Because of an intense patronage battle between the Republican and Democratic organizations lasting from 1967 to 1970, no new judges were appointed for three years. As judgeships became vacant due to death and retirement (and one judge who was found guilty of income-tax evasion), the benches simply remained unoccupied. Democratic Governor Hughes kept naming replacements and the county's Republican state senators kept refusing to approve his nominees; finally, because of the lack of judges, the criminal backlog became so dangerous that Judge Crane attempted to relieve the log jam by closing the courts to civil cases. As a result of the politicians' battle, no citizen of Passaic County could claim damages in an automobile accident, sue for fraud, or generally seek legal protection. (Emergency divorces were permitted.) There were some, however, who enjoyed the moratorium. To them controlling the courts seemed more important than the rights of the 460,000 people of Passaic County.

Just how important can be shown through the DeFranco-Kavanaugh murder trials, perhaps the most complex and perverse cases in the history of American law. The cases lasted from 1966 to 1970, cost an estimated $10 million, and spread a reign of terror that no one connected with them will soon forget. It started in February 1966, when Mrs. Judy Kavanaugh, a twenty-one-year-old Clifton housewife, disappeared. Her half-nude body was later found near her home. Six months later, in Paterson, Johnny "The Walk" DeFranco, a forty-two-year-old hood, heard a knock on his door, stepped out to his porch, and his throat was slit from ear to ear, a job so professionally done that the blood did not splatter his clothes. DeFranco, according to *Look* magazine, was in trouble with his superiors for skimming more than his $1,500 weekly take from a $1-million annual rackets operation, he had been involved in counterfeiting and his associates suspected him of having "squealed" to Secret Service agents.

Thevos eventually placed Joseph Muccio, the county investigator who officially served on the gambling squad and called Bozzo "my dearest friend," in charge of the cases. Muccio had never investigated a murder. He propounded the theory that Mrs. Kavanaugh had been involved in a counterfeiting and pornography ring, was silenced when she panicked, and DeFranco was later killed to keep him silent about her death. Five people were indicted on the charge that they had taken part in the murder of these two panicky co-conspirators in the supposed counterfeiting and pornography enterprises. The defendants included Mrs. Kavanaugh's husband; Harold Matzner, a suburban newspaper publisher for whom Kavanaugh had been working as a truck driver; his wife, Dorothe Matzner; and one of DeFranco's numbers runners. Their connections with the victims were tenuous at best. Matzner's name, for example, had turned up among the hundreds of others found in DeFranco's papers. He explained that he knew the racketeer because he had been paying him for tips on underworld stories. The fifth defendant was John DeGroot, a Clifton, New Jersey, police sergeant who had once refused to tell Muccio the name of a federal informer operating in Passaic County.

The prosecution, in large part, built its case around the testimony of Edward Lenney, another hood who was then serving time and was desperate to get out of prison. Lenney heard he could help himself by claiming a part in the De-Franco murder. He came in contact with Muccio, was granted immunity from prosecution (his armed-robbery sentence was later cut in half), and signed a statement saying he had watched the defendants kill DeFranco. Lenney eventually recanted this story in the presence of a special prosecutor who had been brought in to handle the case. Moreover, nine witnesses placed Lenney in Baltimore the night he claimed to have watched the murder. On the basis of these discrepancies, the special prosecutor asked Thevos to dismiss the indictments. Muccio paid a visit to Lenney and he withdrew his retraction. The cases went to trial. F. Lee Bailey, who was then Matzner's defense attorney, wrote an open letter to every legislator in the state, demanding an investigation of the Passaic County prosecutor's office. "I have never in any state or Federal government court seen abuses of justice, legal ethics and constitutional rights such as this case involved," he noted. The State Supreme Court subsequently forbade Bailey to practice in New Jersey for "unethical conduct." Although the DeFranco trial was the longest in state history, the evidence was so flimsy that the jury acquitted the defendants after a few hours of deliberation. Those of the defendants also accused of Mrs. Kavanaugh's murder were acquitted, as well.

The trials left many questions behind them. Why had the prosecutor's office relentlessly pressed these cases for four years in the face of such tenuous evidence? One defense attorney openly charged the prosecution of having "framed" the defendants. The evidence in Mrs. Kavanaugh's murder pointed toward her having been the random victim of an itinerant dishwasher, and nothing in the background of this suburban housewife indicated that she had been involved in counterfeiting and pornography. The inability to find De-Franco's real murderers is even more interesting. The Paterson police described it as a gangland killing and *Look* magazine later reported having learned that a contract had gone out for his death. But who had executed this contract? At the trial a companion of DeFranco's testified that DeFranco had peeked out the window before opening the door and remarked, "It's two laws." "Laws," he said, could have meant anyone connected with the police, federal or local law-enforcement personnel. The testimony of this particular witness was not entirely credible and it may be that his statement means nothing, but the questions of who killed DeFranco and why *Look* magazine learned about the contract when the prosecutor's office had not, do mean a great deal.

Moreover, the defendants, who spent years contemplating the electric chair, were not the only ones to suffer. Several defense witnesses were charged with perjury. Other witnesses received death threats before testifying. The two Paterson policemen who originally investigated the DeFranco murder, saying it was a gangland case, were indicted for malfeasance in office. Another Paterson policeman, who had quit the case in disgust over the conduct of the prosecutor's office, was later threatened with a murder charge for shooting an armed man threatening a city doctor. An editor of the *Passaic Herald* was fired for backing a reporter who had revealed a discrepancy in the case. The *Morning Call* reporter covering the trials was endlessly harassed.

The practices revealed during these highly publicized trials gave only a surface view of the machine's power. Reporters, policemen, no one could combat the rulers of Passaic County. Against a county that had defeated F. Lee Bailey, what chance was there for a welfare recipient threatened with the loss of his allotment if he voted? If a newspaper publisher with the best legal representation in America could not guarantee his civil rights, who could? For the powerful of Passaic County, Paterson was their most valuable property. The rackets, urban renewal, every kind of venture both public and private flourished there. The suburbs may have been a nicer place to live, but places where people bought their own homes instead of having public housing built for them, did not offer the same opportunities for corruption. Paterson could not be permitted to break away and stand by itself.

*I don't say suppose the right side goes under, I say
suppose all sides are right as it seems to them and
they all blur together and their beliefs grow confused and the pluribus becomes so complicated
and, more important so dense that no human mind
or even group of minds can fathom the unum.*

—JOHN GARDNER
The Sunlight Dialogues *

It was now the fall of 1968, a little over a year and a half since
Kramer had taken office. The city had almost ceased to function. Its court system was cut off because of a dispute between
the county and the state. Federal aid had been halted until
the question of the housing commissioner's ouster was decided. No level of government seemed to offer channels for
constructive change, only cause for frustration. The Citizens'
Advisory Council on Urban Renewal suggested its only logical step was to disband since the Housing Authority paid
no attention to its advice. The county bar association was

* Copyright © 1972 by John Gardner. Reprinted by permission of Alfred A.
Knopf, Inc.

suing the governor and the entire state senate to force them to appoint judges. It was pointed out that even if the bar association won the suit and the courts ordered the governor and senators to act, it would make no difference; the governor could go on indefinitely naming judges and the senators would keep on rejecting them. Kramer had accused the Civil Service Commission of trying to force out Bechtel for political purposes and got nowhere. Threet had not yet finished his three-year struggle to obtain an F.H.A. mortgage to start renovations in the Fourth Ward.

In this atmosphere, where the city could find neither answers nor progress, the flames of the first week of July never quite died and, instead, became smouldering embers. Seared and bewildered, Paterson returned to a public life composed of rage, confusion, and suspicion. "In a city the size of Paterson," as Allen Ginsberg states, "there are maybe 150 people who really know what's going on. They're the ones who are involved in it or who have access to the gossip. As for everyone else, their basic civic relations are cut off. The reality is just the opposite of what the politicians tell them or what the newspapers say. The result is a complete mythification of public consciousness. In the end, people are walking around in the midst of a clearly defined hell. But they can't put their fingers on its causes or structure. Finally, they just decide that life itself is hell." Certainly Paterson had come to this conclusion; and Kramer had to decide to do something about it if he wished to survive.

In many respects, Kramer's original program did not bear on Paterson's real difficulties. He had never given much thought to the urban structure or the position of the cities. For him, practical measures and honesty within the existing structure constituted the solution and only occasionally did he look beyond that. He did, for example, have a feeling for

long-range planning and orderly growth, but it was difficult
for the city to move beyond crisis decision making because
no one knew when money would be coming from the federal
government or the state and in what kind of strung-up
package it would be allocated. The mayor was genuinely
concerned about the city's cultural life and felt it was vital
that the city should be "more than bricks and mortar." One
of his first major projects had been renovating the library
and he was disappointed that there were not more funds
available for such facilities. In other respects, despite the
restrictions that hampered him, he could have proceeded
further. Paterson then, for example, had the first rent-control
statute in New Jersey, which was framed to be enforced
selectively against slumlords. Rent control, however, was too
radical a measure for Kramer and he brushed it aside as "a
fake solution." The police-community relations program was
a beginning for better communication with the police department, but it was certainly not the single action available to
him. Kramer could have made more strenuous efforts to
remove obstructionists from City Hall, but it seemed he had
no desire to risk further confrontations.

Like all mayors, he had to take what was available and
what was available was not designed to meet the city's needs.
He had placed great faith in the conventional solutions,
particularly federal aid, which had only procured the Senior
Citizens Council, the six portable swimming pools, and a few
sundries. The state's greatest contribution could have been
reforming its tax and aid formulas; not even the paltry
$12-million urban-aid package had yet limped its way through
the legislature. As for the county, it had turned its resources
against Paterson generally and Kramer specifically. There
was no help coming from the outside.

Kramer had already met the Waterloo of all reform-
coalition mayors; his election in itself had raised higher

expectations than it was possible to fulfill. Then had come the riot and the raid, which had been for him shocks as profound as they had been for the rest of the city. "Who knows what really caused the Puerto Ricans to go off?" he asked with a sad smile. "You know, I went and talked to those kids myself and they weren't really angry. It's more a breakdown in communications than anger. They said they have nowhere to go and nothing to do. We're building a beautiful new boys' club down the street and they didn't even know about it." As for the raid, "It was so hard to put together," he recalled afterward. "I'd seen the other side of the police so many times, seen them risk their own lives for other people. Certainly no one wanted to believe that this had happened in Paterson." But whatever their reasons or causes, the events themselves made one thing clear: the mayor could no longer postpone an accounting to the public.

Like Paterson itself, Kramer felt surrounded. He saw the specter of his political powerlessness everywhere—in the smashed storefronts along Graham Avenue, in the crumbling tenements Ventrella had declined to order demolished, in the stalled urban-renewal hearings, in the municipal court backup, in the whispers that followed "the boy wonder" through City Hall, where so many of the former mayor's cohorts remained on the Civil Service payroll.

Kramer was not the first mayor to discover that all the carefully researched "white papers" on housing, education, and law enforcement released during the campaign meant little in the real world of political power, Civil Service regulations, and urban impotence. He was not the first mayor to realize that help from the outside was undependable. He was not the first mayor to find that his city, as a U.S. senator remarked of Los Angeles after the Watts riot, did not "stand for a damned thing" in its capacity to forge its own destiny and power to handle its own affairs. The vision of the Paterson

Kramer had won was now a taunting illusion, but he no longer trusted it. He chose, instead, to respond to the Paterson of his opponents, the Paterson of fears, division, and insecurity, and to the conventional dictates of urban power: running the city as a political enterprise rather than as a public enterprise and using the government as a support for himself rather than as a support for the people. Nor was Kramer the first mayor to discover that he needed the help of a friend—and that an enemy could serve a useful purpose.

The real sources of power, inside Paterson, and in the city's dealings with other levels of government, were often so well hidden that, as one reformer stated, "you could just never get to the bottom of it." Why could the city get some programs from the federal government and not others for which it had been begging for years? Why would the state approve some appointments and not others? In Kramer's view, corruption per se was not the greatest problem. "If there was corruption, it stopped when we took office. The real problem in Paterson was power. The word had just gone down the line that Kramer wasn't going to be allowed to do anything. We weren't getting anywhere with the gangbusters approach. About the only thing we had gotten that way was urban renewal and that took two years. Finally, I thought we should talk to some of these people and see if we couldn't get things moving for the good of the city." The mayor did not say who "these people" were, but certain persons in power in Paterson were conspicuous. One, Joseph G. Bozzo, held no elective or appointive position and yet he saw his friends named to important posts by special act of the state legislature. Lawrence F. Kramer, the elected mayor, could not name a head building inspector.

The totality of Joseph G. Bozzo's system was astonishing. He and his Republican organization worked everywhere, with a disciplined thoroughness that even surprised those who were part of his organization. A *Morning Call* editor was once on the phone arranging a bank loan for his daughter's college tuition. A deliveryman overheard him and casually asked how much it cost to send his daughter to college. "Three thousand dollars." Two hours later the man returned. "A great admirer of yours would like to pay for your daughter's college," he announced. "Joseph G. Bozzo." "Well, I refused the offer from The Bozzo Educational Fund," recalled the editor, "but it certainly shows you how they operate. They're just everywhere." The incident also showed Bozzo's uncanny finesse. He knew that every man has a weakness or a need and if that man were in Passaic County, Bozzo was bound to hear about it. He would step in politely with favors. There were no strings attached, no threats. Except, one day his victim would wake up and realize that there were no strings attached because, without his quite being aware of it, Bozzo already had a rope around his neck.

When asked specifically about his relations with Bozzo, Kramer declared that "he never asked me for a favor in his life." The mayor further resented criticism of his increasing closeness to the Republican organization. "I didn't get the city I ran for," he had once remarked quietly. Kramer was heading a city that was both paralyzed and on the verge of anarchy; a few concessions might bring him a measure of power to move forward. His newfound ability to obtain cooperation from various people and agencies may have only been coincidence, but certainly Bozzo's celebrated tact qualified him to run interference for the mayor in many delicate areas.

Much as Paterson could not afford to remain paralyzed, there was a serious question whether it could any better afford the kind of cooperation that was available to it. Kramer's critics, including a few prominent members of his own administration, doubted that this was the only road open to him; cynics further noted that the mayor himself, having lost a lot of support, increasingly needed firm political alliances for the upcoming reelection. In either case, confidence and faith were crucial to the city. The angry reaction to the first sign of reconciliation between Kramer and Bozzo indicated how disturbing this was to many in Paterson. Kramer had named a protégé of the Republican organization to a newly created post with the Board of Education that would handle maintenance and bus contracts. He vehemently denied open charges that he had done so on Bozzo's orders. Nevertheless, Monsignor William Wall and the Reverend Maxwell Tow sent him a sharp letter of protest. "We doubt there can ever again be the trust and hope that marked the advent of your administration," they wrote.

Having found his friend, the mayor did not have to look hard for his enemy. Kramer contended that he had special reason to be bitter about the city's minority population. He felt that he had done more for them than any mayor in the city's history and, instead of being commended, he had been vilified. The City Hall sit-in had particularly offended him. "I always felt I was tricked into that," he maintained. "They promised to remove those cots and they didn't do it. It wouldn't have mattered what I did. They were dying to have that confrontation at any cost. They wanted to be arrested and come out like martyrs." To him this was proof that no action on his part could ever satisfy the blacks, and apparently it also justified his not making further efforts. Except to fulfill his campaign promise to name a Puerto Rican to the Board of Education and to a City Hall post, he did not make any significant minority appointments during the latter half of his term. Nor did he seek out the moderate leadership composed of the substantial black working class, people who were born and raised in Paterson, who owned homes and held a vested interest in peaceful progress.

In truth, neither the mayor nor the minorities possessed a monopoly on virtue. Kramer may have appointed a number of "firsts," but it was window dressing and the blacks knew it. On the other hand, the city's minority leadership had been kept from legitimate influence for so long that they were inexperienced in negotiating. Their encounters with the mayor were emotionally charged and generally unproductive. Kramer simply was the first major official whom they could attack with any potential for response; consequently, their attention to him was excessive. Often the minority leaders seemed to be more interested in augmenting their individual power by outdoing one another in denouncing the mayor rather than in dealing with real problems. The specific rights and wrongs of the sleep-in, for example, paled beside the fact that it had outraged—and frightened—a large segment of the city to the point where the blacks lost public sympathy for more important issues.

Nevertheless, Kramer had known how to find cooperation when he wanted it and had, in fact, received extensive cooperation during the first part of his term, but without doubt, events had trapped him. Once he made it clear that he felt he could not personally take action in the aftermath of the raid, the blacks were so angered that there was no real question of soothing over differences. But an uneasy calm was still possible; if the mayor's office wanted calm, there was little indication. Now Kramer not only ignored the blacks; he began to react to legitimate requests with angry condemnation. On occasion he seemed to be deliberately challenging the blacks to take action against him. Appearing as a guest speaker at the Task Force's annual convention, which was the most important annual gathering in the black community, he blasted the agency's entire program, calling it a waste of time and a waste of money. It was his first speech to a black audience since the raid and he was booed out of the building. This did not seem to disturb the mayor. "I just spoke to them honestly and they didn't like it," he explained.

Kramer's double conversion struck many disquieting chords in Paterson. "When it comes to the hard nuts and bolts, politicians have to go to power. There's nothing else they can do, so he went where it was in Paterson," remarked one observer. "Much as I like Pat Kramer," commented one of his early and most influential supporters, "I can't help but feel that what happened was a tragedy. His position wasn't easy, but people knew what was going on and the city would have stuck with him. For once, Paterson was ready to go the whole way, to throw out that whole crew and he backed down." "He couldn't have won with the blacks no matter what he did," said one priest. "Working on his campaign was the biggest mistake I ever made," said a black teenager.

Tragedy, mistake, necessity? There were clearly no miracles in store for Paterson, but Kramer's new tack nevertheless had profound repercussions. The facts were not so simple that they could be judged solely on questions of power and of right or wrong. Paterson had attempted to raise itself above the level of a commodity to function as a place where its citizens had human dimensions. But the mayor's capitulation returned Paterson to its customary status. The city was no longer a functioning whole; it was once again a series of manipulatable parts where its own interests faded against the interests of its rulers. And once this attitude had regained entrance to the mayor's office, it did not stop there, but seeped through Paterson like acid, opening old wounds and leaving the city raw, divided, and shaken.

Most people in Paterson did not have direct knowledge of the inner workings of government, but the city discerned that it was no longer pursuing the quest to redefine its life. For Paterson, making a serious reassessment of its position was not easy. Paterson only attracted the New York television networks when something spectacular, such as a riot or a gangland murder, occurred. The *News* had switched to backing Kramer, but in-depth reporting still was not its specialty. The *Call* could not keep up with everything; exposés on political deals and police problems only touched the surface of the entire system draining Paterson. In terms of cost and destruction to the city, for instance, housing laws that permitted slumlords to operate were worthy of as much front-page coverage as a riot but state housing laws obviously made uninteresting reading.

Despite an underlying awareness of the foul play that assaulted it from every quarter, Paterson could not entirely accept the evidence; everyone from the most sophisticated to the simplest observers uniformly expressed shock when confronted with unvarnished truth of the reality controlling Paterson. Lawrence F. Kramer on his volunteer efforts to reform urban renewal: "It came as absolutely a revelation to us that our ability to bring pressure on government from the outside was so limited." Florence Brawer on the failure of her group's many investigations to obtain results: "Everywhere we went, the state, the federal government, the power was endless and we'd keep finding more and more connections. People either didn't want to act or they were afraid to act. But, you know, after all we had learned, people still couldn't believe it." Jeff Mallory, a black leader, after the attack on the S.C.L.C.: "I couldn't believe this had happened with what I'd been taught about living in a democracy." An elderly Puerto Rican shouting at the Task Force board of directors after it decided to take over the Spanish antipoverty program: "That's not democracy. Where does our voice come in? Where's the democracy?"

Just as Kramer returned to the traditional method of ruling the city by division, Paterson fell back to its traditional mistrust, insecurities, and the "conspiracy" view of its troubles. Suspicion for every event in the city's life focused on a malignant "them." When some merchants banded together to protect themselves from robberies, the blacks accused them of being the vanguard of a vigilante movement. One of Kramer's kindliest aides mistakenly assumed that a special school some blacks had started for dropouts was formulated to be what he called a "hate school." Although the civil-rights leaders had, when called, cooperated with the police in trying to calm the riot, many of the police brass never stopped believing that they were the ones who had instigated it. And many black leaders never stopped believing that their lives were in constant danger, although, in their case, the mysterious shots fired from passing cars confirmed this belief.

In the period following the raid and the riot, the city probably experienced its most intense level of public activism since the Great Strike. Everyone had a cause; groups on all sides pressed their views. Most of this activism was wasted. The city's valuable qualities—its persistent if sometimes clumsy vitality, its courage, its desire to do things "the right way"—could find no outlets for change through conventional methods—through voting or the courts or peaceful approaches to officials. These invariably met rebuffs. So Paterson returned to the old quarrels of people who felt, whatever their individual viewpoints, that their only chance lay in protecting their own positions—at any cost.

A short time after the riot, a pleasant-faced woman whose plumpness was beginning to affirm her middle age stopped

by City Hall to watch the urban-renewal hearings while
waiting for her bus. At that moment in the proceedings, Raff
had been droning on for several hours. Two of the elderly
Finance Board commissioners had fallen asleep and were
snoring lightly. Raff's co-counsel leafed through a newspaper
and City Counsel Conn sat at the table in the front of the
room flanked by two awake and two drowsing commissioners;
he drummed the table absentmindedly as if he despaired of
ever forcing Raff to stop talking. John Wegner sat at another
table while a handful of reporters and spectators watched
silently.

It seemed impossible that the actions of these people,
awake, asleep, fidgeting, and reading newspapers, should
stand between Paterson and $32 million in federal aid. The
pleasant-faced woman started talking with another spectator.
She was bored and disgusted and greatly wanted to define her
uneasiness. Her feelings did not stem specifically from the
hearings, although the scene before her was hardly reassur-
ing; like many in Paterson, she simply felt an incessant urge
to discuss the events of the past few months as if somehow
a reason or an answer would appear. The other spectator
asked her who she was voting for in the presidential election.
"I'm going Wallace. A lot of people are going Wallace.
I worked in the Kramer campaign and I learned. You can't
make politics honest." She had other remarks on the administration. "There's too many liberals. The Democrats and the
Republicans are all mixed up together. It doesn't make sense.
I like things that make sense. During the riot, Kramer went
and asked the Puerto Ricans what they wanted. That's not
the way to do it. You tell them what they've got." She lit a
cigarette and pointed out her complaints. She could barely
pay her taxes. She was afraid to send her twelve-year-old
daughter to the public schools but didn't have money for a
private school. Others received presents from the government.

"They got all those pools this summer and they slashed them up. They're not grateful. It's a waste of money. Nobody's doing anything for the taxpayer. We need law and order."

When asked if she thought Wallace might not cause worse riots than those so far, her answer expressed the real longing of everyone in Paterson from Klan members to those with a welfare allotment. "Well, good then. Let's get it decided. Things need to come to a head. You can't just go on drifting this way."

The Taxpayers Association, composed of conservative, concerned, and honest whites, represented one group that was determined not to let things "go on drifting." Thomas C. Rooney, Jr., its forty-two-year-old president, was at first regarded as an eccentric do-gooder with a notion of saving the city overnight. He had run for mayor as an independent in 1966 and had received 368 votes. But the intense, dark-haired TV repairman had risen considerably in stature since then. He opposed welfare and tax increases for any purpose, and constantly called for stringent honesty. He toted his lists of useless patronage jobs, welfare statistics, law-and-order petitions, slides of various "disgraceful" areas of the city, charts, graphs, and illustrations of Paterson's "terrible decay" to board meetings, public debates, P.T.A.'s—wherever he could find an audience large or small. In a way, his supporters had much in common with the blacks; both distrusted government, were fed up with corruption, and lived to some extent as outsiders from the city's life.

Rooney's analysis of the city was straightforward: The politicians made up programs solely to spend money and gain power. Then they raised taxes to make the homeowners pay for their schemes. Rooney would end all programs and thus stop the rise in taxes; he would refuse all new welfare cases except for the disabled and elderly. Rooney intended to investigate every welfare case. "Paterson has seventy-eight percent of the county welfare load," he pointed out. "Is this fair? Is this right? No, sir. How is it possible for one city to have 4,000 missing fathers?" And he felt the city had to have law and order or it would be destroyed. "This has nothing to do with race," noted Rooney, who once said he would order the police to shoot his own brother for throwing a firebomb. "People in every section of this town live in fear. This is not a normal way to live. It is not civilized. It is wrong."

Rooney's admirers grew daily. They were not people who ordinarily took part in politics; they were driven by the feeling that, while being forced to finance everyone from welfare recipients to building contractors, they received nothing. It is interesting, for example, to look at the relations between the Taxpayers Association, the chief spokesman for small homeowners in Paterson, and urban renewal, the single federal program (until the recent advent of revenue sharing) supposedly designed to help the urban middle class. The Taxpayers Association did not think that office buildings were going to aid its members. On the contrary, the association vehemently opposed renewal and denounced the $32-million program as simply another waste of money and a contributing factor to the distress of its members.

The interests of the association, under any conditions, would have conflicted with those of other groups. Rooney himself could not understand the toll that institutionalized prejudice had taken on the blacks. To him, blacks were being treated equally if there were competent white administrators in the schools and he had no sympathy for ideas such as making special efforts to promote minority administrators. The association had done some hard-core constructive work, such as investigating the schools, but in a situation where no level of government seemed to recognize the needs or existence of ordinary urban homeowners, its members were driven to a state of alienation. The association deteriorated into a program based not on reforms but on reprimands, regarding any city action—urban renewal, pay raises for teachers, negotiations with the minorities—as a subterfuge designed to hurt taxpaying homeowners. As a result of its endless protests, its much-needed cry for decency was often drowned in the countercry of the many groups who regarded the association as a direct threat.

Although Rooney considered politics an immoral occupation, he had once run for mayor out of his "duty to serve the city" and announced his intention to try again. In the various wreckages that Kramer had left behind him, he also started attracting some of the mayor's rabidly idealistic supporters. By the fall of 1968 after the riot, the Taxpayers Association's protests had reached a pitch where it was attacking the administration in apocalyptic terms. When, for example, Kramer approved some minor tax abatements for much-needed middle-class housing, the association took out newspaper ads that read in part: "Why, Mayor Kramer, are you promoting two entirely different systems of taxation in the city. . . . How extremely unfair this is! How foreign to our American tradition of fair and equal taxation for everyone! We will prove it is extremely harmful, totally unfair, inherently evil, and will necessarily destroy our city!"

As much as the Taxpayers Association regarded the administration's least action as "inherently evil," its stand was benign compared to that of another group. There was one place where Kramer would never be forgiven: the Fourth Ward.

Broadway stretches out from Main Street at a right angle. Between the downtown commercial area and the ghetto there are a few blocks of no-man's-land. Many of the small stores are deserted and occasionally the owners have left behind traces of their bitterness at being forced by robberies, unpaid bills, and dwindling customers to abandon their businesses. "Goodbye, Paterson. We couldn't wait for you to move, so we are moving," reads one sign in an empty window. Further along Broadway one arrives at "antipoverty row." Tucked away on either side of the street are the modern brick and glass Task Force building, the storefront Model Cities office, the Paterson Street Academy for dropouts, the New Tenants Union, and an abandoned church, which the Kramer administration converted into the Martin Luther King Community Center.

This is the Fourth Ward. It is slum-ridden, crime-ridden, drug-ridden, and at the same time it is the most "governed" area of Paterson. It receives welfare from the county, the Community Center from the city, the Street Academy from the state, the Task Force and Model Cities from the federal government, and a variety of other programs and projects. It receives more law-enforcement "attention" than any other part of Paterson. The Fourth Ward, in short, is the ultimate creation of the urban structure. Through drugs and the rackets, it is the most valuable area of the city to organized crime. The machine's survival in large part rests on its ability to manipulate the Fourth Ward. It is the place where the federal government proves its "involvement" in the cities. The Fourth Ward is told how to live most aspects of its life; its young ladies are instructed how to put on their makeup at the federally sponsored Charm Center and its adults are instructed how they should vote. The Fourth Ward, indeed, has everything except the right to conduct its own affairs.

It would be interesting to know to what extent the systematic assault on individual integrity in the Fourth Ward feeds on itself, breeding more crime and violence, more people on welfare. What, for example, does it do a child's perception of the real responsibilities of adulthood to see his parents treated always like children, always controlled by other adults? How much of the dehumanization is enforced from the outside? Jane Jacobs quotes from a settlement-house report that shows how the bureaucratic bullying of tenants in public housing projects destroys even the most natural and casual human contacts:

> To protect themselves, they [the tenants] make few, if any, friends. Some are afraid that friends will become angry or envious and make up a story to report to management, causing them great trouble. . . . For these families, the sense of privacy has already been extensively violated. The deepest secrets, all the family skeletons, are well known not only to management but often to other public agencies such as the Welfare Department. To preserve any last remnants of privacy, they chose to avoid close relationships with others. . . . Even in England, this suspicion of neighbors and ensuing aloofness was found in studies of planned towns. Perhaps this pattern is nothing more than an elaborate group mechanism to protect and preserve inner dignity in the face of so many outside pressures to conform.*

Some urban theorists, raking over the coals of the 1960s and the failure of poverty programs, are baffled as to what "special approach" can next be taken with the ghettos. There are, without doubt, special conditions in the Fourth Ward that require attention. Like most urban slums, it has a high proportion of teenagers and a consequent need for organized recreational activities. It has addicts who should be treated. Its large number of migrants probably necessitates local community-action programs or some other means guiding people through the complexities of urban life. But, as always, the most important question for the Fourth Ward is how can

* From *The Death and Life of Great American Cities.* Copyright © 1961 by Jane Jacobs. Reprinted by permission of Random House, Inc.

it direct its resources toward the needs and interests of its citizens? This does not seem to be a question that concerns any level of government. It is perhaps easiest to illustrate the frustrations, bitterness, and waste of its talents and aspirations by taking a look at the career of Mrs. Bessie Jamieson.

Mrs. Jamieson, a serious, pleasant-looking woman with a tough appreciation for power, first emerged as part of a group seeking a modest $70,000 rehabilitation project from the county after the 1964 riot. The county did not dare refuse outright its support. The Board of Freeholders, therefore, approved the plan, let the organizers proceed with their work, and, some months later, announced that, while it may have approved the plans, it had never voted a budget allocation to implement them. Mrs. Jamieson turned from asking to the ballot. In 1965, after a fierce fight, she and a co-runner managed to unseat the white man who had been ward leader of the black Fourth Ward for twenty-six years. Following this, she attempted to push Grossi into putting up more black candidates in the 1966 elections by threatening to lead the Fourth Ward in a revolt from the organization. The prospect of the blacks' acting independently panicked the machine. Instead of negotiating with Mrs. Jamieson, Grossi and the Democratic party just ignored her. The white was brought back, and anyone who wanted attention from government agencies and other services that ward leaders traditionally supply had to go to him.

Meanwhile, the federal government decided to take an interest in the Fourth Ward and started the Task Force, which received $5½ million in four years, more money per capita than any O.E.O. outlet in New Jersey or $70 a year for every officially poor person in Paterson.* The sudden

---

* It seems probable that Paterson received this disproportionate amount of money because Dr. Kenneth Marshall, the Task Force's first director, was formerly the head of HARYOU-ACT in New York and constituted a "name"

availability of federal millions staggered the black community. The Task Force presented the blacks with their first power base and the struggle to control it became the driving force of almost every minority leader in the city. The Task Force did undertake some commendable work, including a Head Start center, legal services, and a job-training program which was once selected as a national model for excellence. (It later fell apart in a bad-check scandal.) But its potential effectiveness was devastated by the power struggle, which was so bitter that four paid directors in four years resigned. By the fourth year, in fact, no black in the city was willing to run for president of the Task Force's board of directors, which constituted the most prestigious honorary post in the black community. (The last said his post had brought him threats on his life from critics within the community.)

How could this disintegration have been avoided when the frustrations of the blacks were so intense? They simply had had no channels of influence other than the Task Force. The ballot had not worked, and in a city where the mayor's office controlled all major appointments they could not gain recognition in municipal government. The federal government had not even assured residents of the Fourth Ward of their voting rights. On top of the disappointment engendered by the fiascos at the Task Force, during this interim all other issues were forgotten. Except for Threet, no one paid much attention to housing. Although more than half the voters in the Fourth Ward were unregistered, voter-registration drives were rare. Even critical problems such as drug addiction were ignored as the Fourth Ward's leadership fought over the Task Force. By 1968 the fact that Paterson did not have one public drug treatment center (although the state had agreed

in the relatively new business of fighting poverty. Marshall had also blasted the late Adam Clayton Powell for using HARYOU-ACT politically, which may have made him a favored person in federal eyes.

to reimburse counties for seventy-five percent of the costs for drug treatment) was attributable to the county's negligence. But no one appeared at the Board of Freeholders to demand a program, and finally the county started a "part-time" program the following year.

By the fall of 1968 Mrs. Jamieson was firmly in command as vice-president of the Task Force and headed the Federation of Neighborhood Councils, its community organizing arm. An ally of hers would soon take over as paid director. Mrs. Jamieson had not forgotten how the Fourth Ward had once succumbed to threats and cheap favors, but now it was Mrs. Jamieson who was in a position to hand out favors and she had determined that the Task Force should have the strength to be recognized as an undisputed power in Paterson. The agency brought many other groups under its sphere of influence; Black Panthers and N.A.A.C.P. members alike found spots on the payroll as "organizers" and "aides." The Task Force, in short, had become the "official" spokesman for minority Paterson. In the face of the various scandals that had plagued its operations, the white community had difficulty accepting it as a serious voice. The number of demonstrations that blacks themselves had held against it indicated that they did not accept the Task Force as their sole representative. But the Task Force had found the only apparent means to become a voice in Paterson—money and well-applied power.

Then had come the raid that had totally unbalanced the Fourth Ward. Kramer's reaction infuriated them. The blacks had expected better of him, not only because he had seemed to promise better, but because, as Kramer himself knew, the support he had received from the Fourth Ward had often required courage to give. Jeff Mallory, the tall, heavy-set vice-president of the S.C.L.C., had been one of those trapped inside the S.C.L.C. headquarters during the raid, choking on tear gas and thinking, "this was going to be my last day on earth." He, too, had once been an ardent Kramer supporter and, like many, felt that the mayor's declining to take personal action after the raid was a deliberate betrayal of the Fourth Ward. "You could say I worked my natural cakes off for that man," Mallory commented. "I was out all the time, talking to people, trying to convince them that it was worth a try, that here was somebody who was going to do something. I even pasted his pictures all over the store, knowing what this town was like, and that I'd be under the gun if he lost." The mayor had not responded in kind.

Where was the Fourth Ward to take its anger and bitter disappointment? The city had already said it would not act; the county and the federal governments had started hesitant, tedious investigations that eventually got nowhere. The Fourth Ward once again was left with no outlet but to turn in on itself, and the Task Force, as its official voice, led the way. Fighting white injustices had proved fairly futile, but it was determined at least to "unite" the minorities through the device of suppressing anything it could not control. The first showdown came with the Hispanic groups. The Task Force had previously allocated the Spanish a relatively small amount of money to run their own program in conjunction with the archdiocese of Paterson. It remained the single poverty program not under the Task Force's direct control, and the tie with the archdiocese was particularly galling because the Church had just tranferred out of Paterson a militant priest who had given the blacks strong support. The Task Force "investigated" the program, pronounced it "a glorified, paternalistic welfare system," and moved to retake it.

The Spanish and Puerto Rican groups, who had little interest in the blacks' quarrels with the archdiocese and regarded this as their program, were alarmed into their greatest show of solidarity. They ironed out an agreement for running the program and vowed to defend it. Armed with their agreement, several hundred followers, and a petition containing 2,000 signatures supporting their position, the Spanish appeared at a meeting of the Task Force board of directors. The directors declined to read the Spanish agreement and promptly voted to take over the program. (One former Task Force official had foreseen the appearance of large numbers of Puerto Ricans at the meeting. He owned a funeral home in his private business and occupied himself by handing out flyers to the angry and disappointed crowd. The flyers bore the announcement, "Nosotros Transportamos Cadavres a Puerto Rico" ("We Fly Bodies to Puerto Rico"). As a result, any chance for a much-needed black-Spanish coalition in Paterson was destroyed.

No sooner had the Task Force written off the Spanish and apparently become the master of minority Paterson than a new threat appeared. In October, after a year of begging the federal government, Kramer managed to obtain a Model Cities grant which was then estimated to bring $25 million to the Fourth Ward, although this figure was later slashed by the federal government. Yet so intense was the opposition to Kramer that many blacks were willing to turn back $25 million rather than see him make progress. The mayor received an angry telegram: "We are pledged to close down the Model Cities program before we will relinquish its control to boondogglers and have it run by phonies and hustlers," concluded the ten signers. The mayor sarcastically referred to the telegram as being from "Bessie's boys." Many of the signers were on the Task Force payroll and they next asked the Department of Housing and Urban Development for "an immediate suspension" of Model Cities. Although Model Cities overcame this attack, these endless battles bled the city's energy and good will.

Back at the voting booth, the Democratic organization, in a burst of subtlety, had realized that the way to handle the Fourth Ward was not by reinstalling whites, but by installing blacks it could live with. The Fourth Ward now had its own ward leader, alderman, and assemblyman; but it was rare to see them at the board of education, the police board, or the Board of Freeholders, pointing out the facts of life in Paterson.

In between lay a community disillusioned with Kramer, disappointed with the Task Force, disgusted with the political organizations—and lacking the means to control its existence.

Two ounces of protein food, ½ pint of whole milk, ¾ cup of fruit and/or vegetable, a slice of enriched bread or its equivalent, a teaspoon of butter or margarine.

—U.S. DEPARTMENT OF AGRICULTURE
Guidelines for a school lunch

In the confusion that followed the shattering events of July 1968, emotional and political confrontation centered on these two issues: Paterson's police and its schools. Disappointment and anger may have arisen over other issues, but to the "average" citizen the schools and the police constituted familiar scapegoats for venting their sense of powerlessness and distrust of government. The public's response to these two institutions gave the best indication of the city's mood and of the desperate, but usually futile, attempts of its citizens to find a means of holding on to the things closest to them.

The condition of the police and the schools best illustrates the startling absence of public accountability resulting from the city's heritage and structure. While city agencies are never entirely free from questions of power and politics, the schools and the police were embroiled in these matters to the extent that they meant more than the performance of their civic duties; they were seen, not as public agencies, but as servers or protectors of the city's rulers. Their insulation was partly the result of organizational arrangements; all the police and school commissioners were political appointees, and Civil Service regulations gave ironclad protection to incompetence. But Paterson's difficulties with its schools and police were not unusual; the problem clearly went deeper.

Whatever their importance to the public, the schools and police, both wracked by scandals for a century, had traditionally been the two municipal agencies most vital to the city's potentates. Was there much difference between the onetime police action against a factory workers' strike and now against civil-rights advocates? Was there a difference between a workers' strike over the sole demand that their children should be educated and the blacks' boycott of schools that were indifferent to their children? The law-enforcement machinery was crucial to whoever ruled the city; the Board of Education, with the largest budget in the city, had been a fertile source of building contracts and patronage. Both responded first to the dictates of power.

On the evening of September 5, 1968, two months after the riot, the nine-member Paterson Board of Education prepared to convene its first public meeting of the school year. The school year had started abnormally, accompanied by a boycott and tension and anger. Several months before, the Task Force had sent the Board of Education nineteen demands, the first of which was that Superintendent Michael Gioia be fired because he "does not possess either the ability or the desire" to provide educational leadership; other demands included more minority teachers, community control, and a hot-lunch program in ghetto schools. The blacks were further angered that federal Title I money, which is supposed to be earmarked for "disadvantaged" children, had been used in the board's regular budget. (Apparently this was a standard fate of Title I money throughout the country, but the Department of Health, Education and Welfare had made no protest.) The board had promised to deal with all the demands—except Gioia's dismissal—over the summer, but it had made slow progress in implementing changes. It also had not extended the blacks a report on its intentions and had not included the Task Force's demands in the "official agenda" of its first fall meeting. With only one black commissioner to represent nearly half the city, the board perhaps was not well informed about the mood of the minorities.

In response to the board's inaction, the Task Force called a school boycott. General annoyance prevailed in the city at the specter of the schools' opening surrounded by police and the apparent indifference of city officials. Neither the board nor the superintendent's office had made a substantial effort to smooth over trouble spots; in fact, Dr. Gioia, who was earning $32,300 a year, making him the highest-paid official in Paterson, had gone on vacation during the rising crisis in August and then dropped out of sight on an indefinite sick leave. (He later explained that he was the victim of an undisclosed critical illness.) The official indifference reached such proportions that the nonpartisan League of Women Voters finally sent a delegation to the mayor, requesting that he assert leadership over educational matters one way or the other. Kramer merely responded by saying that some of the Task Force's demands were just, some weren't, and declined to elaborate further.

At the opening meeting, a capacity crowd filed into the board meeting room. Mrs. Marian Rauschenbach, a fragile-

looking woman, presided. A longtime civic leader and early
Kramer supporter, Mrs. Rauschenbach found the board
meetings increasingly disturbing. She sought to impose discipline by strictly following Robert's Rules of Order and
studiously ignoring outbursts from the audience. Ordinarily
Dr. Gioia sat on her right, but since he wasn't there, the education commissioners ranged themselves on either side and
the board attempted to begin its regular agenda. The meetings customarily started with a half hour of tedium—reading resolutions, assigning administrators, granting cafeteria
workers leaves of absence—and then proceeded to the clerk's
reading of the uniformly hostile letters from parents, which
expressed anger over nonexistent supplies, unheated buildings, and other matters. After the clerk read each letter in
an expressionless voice, a hush fell over the audience as the
crowd waited to hear Mrs. Rauschenbach's response. Those
parents and community leaders who habitually attended
board meetings had been disappointed a hundred times, but
still they remained expectant, wondering if, once, one letter
would cause Mrs. Rauschenbach to deviate from her standard
comment. It had never happened. After each letter, the president said exactly three words: "Received and filed." Following these preliminaries, the public was allowed to speak—on
any subject that the board had included in "the official
agenda."

On the evening of September 5, however, the board did
not even make its way unscathed through the rhythmic security of "receiving and filing" its mail. A few moments after
the commissioners started taking resolutions on personnel
assignments, Richie Sargeant, a young black, and a group of
supporters marched into the back of the room. "Paterson!
Oh, Paterson! Hear, hear!" they shouted. Sargeant, well
known locally as the former head of CORE and a sometime
militant, had, as a "goodwill" gesture, been hired by the city

during the summer to protect the six portable swimming pools, which vandals slashed anyway. This evening he and his followers, aside from challenging the board, were publicly introducing African dress to Paterson and were carefully arranging themselves in single file to display their brightly colored robes and dashikis.

The Sargeant group had waited for a particular moment to make its entrance—when the board would appoint Joseph Farrell as director of the Bureau of Special Services. The Bureau of Special Services oversaw "disruptive" children. The black community felt that Special Services was less a remedial program than a device to segregate black children and one that prejudiced teachers used to remove black children from their classrooms. The audience immediately questioned Farrell's qualifications to work with disturbed children. Mrs. Rauschenbach noted that the state Office of Special Education had screened the applicants.

"Then I am correct that the good doctor, with all deference to him, has no experience in dealing with deprived children," one man commented.

Sargeant next stepped forward and demanded recognition. "I'm sure the older members of the Board of Education have never seen a congregation like this," he began. "The reason is that the people of Paterson want better education. Is that true?"

"Amen, amen," replied his followers.

"I think you've made your point. Have you finished, Mr. Sargeant?" inquired Mrs. Rauschenbach.

"No, I haven't," said Sargeant. "If the white people of Paterson won't change the system, then the black people will. We are absolutely fed up with politics' directing education." The board promptly passed the appointment and the Sargeant group stalked out. "Well, at least we made our thing," one muttered.

The board's next order of business concerned School 22, the school for children in need of special services. The board decided to transfer some of its classes to a church basement. No explanation was offered for what could be better accomplished in a church basement, but the board apparently felt it had to make some response to the insistent criticism of School 22 and transferring classes was the only device it had been able to think of. The community's main concern, on the other hand, was how children were selected to be sent to the school. "Are they tested before they're sent there?" demanded one man, and the audience took up a spontaneous cry of "No, no, no." One mother jumped from her front-row seat. "They took my kid," she screamed, "and they didn't give him no testing! I went twelve times and they tell me they ain't got time."

With the formal portion of the evening over, the meeting turned into a free-for-all. The blacks demanded to know what had happened to their demands and Mrs. Rauschenbach pointed out that they couldn't be discussed since they weren't on the official agenda. The board vice-president, Jerome Levine, intervened and cited the progress in naming minority administrators, training teachers' aides, and the promise to proceed with the hot-lunch program as soon as cost estimates were completed. Thomas Rooney, representing the Taxpayers Association, presented his own "requests, not demands." He requested that the board not negotiate under threats, investigate the legality of the Task Force's sponsoring a boycott with federal funds, and that it should take action to force parents to send their children to school as required by law. The clamor following his statement gave the board an opportunity to pass unobtrusively its final resolution—adjournment of the meeting.

The crowd filed out, the commissioners left, the clerk gathered up the officially received and filed letters, and the meeting, during which only angry exchanges had passed between the commissioners and the audience, was over. In the midst of the shouting and accusations, one elderly man had stood up, looked the board members calmly in the face, and, speaking with a deliberate slowness, fingered the deadly flaw. "As we say on the corners, you ain't been minding your business. Now I'll translate that for you intellectuals. It means you haven't put enough time, enough care, or enough concern into the board."

The debate over urban education is endless: Are the schools themselves a failure or is it that urban children "can't learn" due to environmental factors beyond the control of the schools? Yet the whole system is so illegitimate—its curriculum decided by suburban state legislators, its administration convulsed by politics and power struggles between teachers, parents, and other groups, its students perhaps the last consideration—that there is no real criterion for measuring its performance. That there are children in every society who shouldn't be in a "normal" classroom is undeniable; but that the United States, with the most expensive public education system in the world, should have turned out twenty-one million functional illiterates is absurd. Even the failure of special projects can hardly be taken as proof that there is nothing the schools can do; for a child to receive a good teacher or be part of an "enriched" program for a year or two is not enough to make up for the other years of hostility, apathy, and mismanagement that generally describe the urban school experience.

In 1969 a group in Paterson conducted a highly controlled experimental summer program, which gave a startling idea of the schools' insularity from their pupils. A group of 240 Spanish children, chosen for their general intractability, poor attendance, and academic failure, were placed in bilingual classes for six weeks. The program, whose results attracted national attention, was designed to improve their language ability and heighten their self-esteem through their culture and heritage. The children maintained an unbelievable ninety-one percent daily attendance record and improved their reading scores in both Spanish and English by twenty percent. (A recreational day camp run by the same group had a much lower attendance record, indicating perhaps how anxious "deprived" children are to find structured, constructive uses for their time.) Their major problem was that they had not understood English well enough to cooperate in their regular classes. As a result, the board of education and the superintendent's office started to express cautious interest in bilingual education.

Even with increased awareness of cultural barriers and language difficulties, the urban schools have not seriously confronted these problems. This failure results partly from the fact that, just as the cities as a whole do not have commensurate influence in the outside world, likewise urban school systems receive short shrift. State boards of education set standards and state legislatures pass laws regulating their conduct. These standards, oriented toward the suburbs, cover everything from curriculum to requiring high schools to be built on eight acres of land—an extravagant New Jersey law which has left crowded cities with the choices of not building, invading their parks, or tearing down housing.

On the other hand, the states rarely recognize the needs of urban children through measures such as requiring bilingual instruction or including material on "the contributions of minority groups" in the curriculum. Local bureaucracies rarely find the courage or inspiration to proceed beyond that which is required by law; thus it is vital that the states mandate change. Even with indisputable evidence of the value of bilingual education, the Paterson board moved slowly because non-Spanish parents opposed instruction in Spanish as being somehow un-American. The newspapers were inundated with letters, such as one from a man who said he arrived in the United States from Italy in 1897, learned English by reading translations of opera librettos, and felt "every child has the same opportunity." The New Jersey legislature, typically indifferent, seems only to have specifically noticed the urban situation on one occasion, when it passed a law forbidding public schools to fly Afro-American or "freedom" flags.

Inexorably intertwined in the power structure and struggle of the cities, urban schools have become another branch in the system of patronage and controls. This struggle does not exist in the suburbs, where the schools (discounting a few routine services such as road maintenance) are the sole *raison d'être* for government, receiving careful attention from the public and local officials. It seems doubtful that a suburban mayor who involved the schools in politics for his own purposes or regarded them as a low item in his own and budgetary priorities would be successful at the polls. However, where the complexities of urban government provide a screen, dozens of mayors, liberal and conservative alike, take this attitude and suffer relatively small consequences. In the cities, political organizations, already systematized in a way they are not in the suburbs, have a notable influence on the schools. The politicians are followed by the teachers and professionals. Tying for last place are the parents, allotted the dubious honor of paying for a system that is almost entirely out of their hands, and the students.

In Paterson the board's primary public relationship is with the mayor, who appoints its members. (It is significant, again, that while many of Paterson's surrounding suburbs have elective boards, the city's members are named solely by the mayor.) Kramer, like many mayors, regarded education as an undertaking fraught with conflicts, demands, and frustrations, and with few guarantees for improvement no matter what "practical solutions" were sought. His highest hope seems to have been that the schools would remain reasonably quiet. At one point he commissioned a professional consultant's report recommending consolidation of the system into middle schools both to upgrade facilities and save money. To the many parents who raised an outcry, this signified busing and the report was quietly buried. Already embroiled in conflicts with the police and urban-renewal authorities, Kramer understandably showed little inclination to move on another front, but his efforts to keep the schools under control by avoiding action ultimately resulted in a deadening paralysis. His reluctance to contend with the school's educational and social conflicts did not mean, however, that he, like most mayors of the city, was equally reluctant to use them politically. As a result, the schools became perhaps the greatest failure of his administration.

Although membership on the board was a nonpaying public-service post, it was coveted by those wishing to launch their careers and had been a traditional dumping ground for political debts. As a consequence, the board was generally mistrusted by the public. Under constant attack, it was not proficient in carrying out routine duties and became paralyzed during periods of crisis. Aside from holding public meetings to receive its regular doses of condemnation, the board had also to decide serious questions such as programs for disturbed and retarded children and general curriculum. Its $18-million budget demanded that the board have some knowledge of business management, union contracts, how to coordinate hundreds of employees and distribute millions of dollars of supplies. As board vacancies became free during his term, Kramer sought to keep long-standing controversies from erupting by appointing "safe" commissioners, i.e., those who generally would not take the board on an independent course. As a gesture toward the Republican organization, Kramer had, for one example, named George Sokalski to the board. Described by the *Morning Call* as "a classic party hack [whose] lack of fresh ideas is startling in a man who has been on various public payrolls for so long," Sokalski was placed in charge of contract negotiations and promised the teachers a wage increase that had not been authorized by the full board. After this offer was withdrawn, Paterson had its first teachers' strike.

On the other hand, Mrs. Rauschenbach, the president, a woman with an impressive record of public service and a member of many civic-improvement organizations had no personal ambitions and did devote time and care to the board. Nevertheless, she served mayoral purposes, if unwittingly. She was not, as one newspaper columnist noted, the type to undertake "a revolt against the head man," and even when she disagreed with Kramer in private, she did not openly advocate educational policy's being decided in its own right, rather than being a branch of politics. Her own gentility perhaps prevented her from fully recognizing the bitterness and outrage that were convulsing the school systems. For example, when one of the high schools broke out in boycotts and violence, Mrs. Rauschenbach gave a short, almost apologetic speech on what she called "youthful, ebullient spirits," which marked her single personal policy statement of the year. "As one observes their [the teenagers'] frustrations," she related, "one wonders how they control their pent-up feelings. How adequate are our facilities when it comes to the average student who wants to toss a basketball in the winter, to practice an instrument, to study quietly, to contemplate? Young people have told me that they cannot study at night because their pent-up energy doesn't let them. Let us build up in our physical-fitness programs, outdoor education week-ends, individual and body-contact sports," she concluded, so every teenager can find "a dignified life as tomorrow's outstanding citizen."

Later a black student plaintively asked the board what action the students could take in the face of adults who showed no apparent interest in them. In reply, Mrs. Rauschenbach asked him if he thought the schools had enough gym space. The young man quickly sat down, not in anger, but in bewilderment. He did not understand what gym space had to do with the students' charges of prejudiced teachers and inferior education. That young man, however, was not the first to falter; no one could dislike Mrs. Rauschenbach, and anger directed against her customarily slithered into an oblivion of incomprehension. For the mayor this produced the convenient effect of making it difficult for critics to focus blame for the educational mess.

Besides the mayor's and the board's lack of leadership, the school administration reflected the public callousness that develops when officials know they are free from acountability. Superintendent Michael Gioia, white-haired, with a weak, nervous smile, had been, as the *Morning Call* put it, "in retreat" for some years. Gioia could rarely be reached by his own staff, the general public, the press, or even, on occasion, by the mayor. The demands for his dismissal, he said, "shocked" him; and, after returning from his three-and-a-half-month leave of absence, he seemed to have taken an interest in new programs such as bilingual instruction, and made Paterson the first city in the state to start teaching children to read in kindergarten. Criticism, however, was still vociferous, particularly concerning his inaccessibility. Board members and administrators privately complained futilely. Indeed, it surprised many people that Gioia wished to remain at a post that apparently made him so uncomfortable.

"Please, sir, if you can't do the job," one parent begged at a board meeting, "just say so and let somebody who wants to take over." But because calling for a new superintendent meant openly acknowledging the mess in the schools, not one person in a position of public responsibility dared suggest it. Through an all too common "balance of power" in the cities, one man, a constant object of attack and dissatisfaction, continued to supervise the education of 26,000 children.

The administrative staff was no more responsive. Gioia himself admitted that the administrators, for the most part, were not prepared to deal with new educational developments. They suffered from a general lack of independence, creativity, and leadership, in part the result of Paterson's method of deciding promotions. The board made up and graded all tests. The schools did not have one black administrator, which the minorities charged was a direct outcome of the tests' being "nothing more than a device to let Dr. Gioia pick who he wants." It also seems to have been a device that helped keep criticism at a comfortably low level. Like the board members, the school's administrative personnel did not complain publicly or seek reform.

Gioia consistently explained that there was no money for the changes and programs he knew were needed. However, new programs and new buildings could hardly erase the entire system's failure or its indifference toward the children in its charge. "You know, I always felt these schools were insensitive to black kids," noted one critic, "but one day, a new thought came to me. They're just as insensitive to white kids." Everything was wrong, from the way supplies were purchased to such a lack of concern that prejudice was blatant. For example, nearby Paterson State College, in trying to increase its own minority enrollment, asked the Paterson schools to recommend qualified blacks. "We don't get much cooperation," an official noted. "The feeling in the Paterson Guidance Departments seems to be that blacks belong in vocational schools or colleges in the South."

This tense atmosphere was probably as influential in causing the schools to flounder as any inadequacies of instruction and programming. In view of the hostility that pervaded the system—the anger of the parents, the disgust of the teachers, the callousness of the administrators—the sometimes hostile attitude of the students was hardly surprising. There were, no doubt, some children beyond the reach of a public-school setting, but hundreds more, capable of learning, were lost through indifference. The tension served to escalate student unrest. The adults' offenses had been so blatant—the purchasing presentment, the political manipulation, the teachers' staging an illegal strike—that the students had become acutely aware of being used and, as became evident later in the year, deeply resented it. The Paterson schools had been teaching their students lessons other than reading and writing for a long time.

The problems facing the schools in a city such as Paterson, where disparate groups are competing for inadequate money, supplies, and attention, were bound to generate conflicts in any case, but official callousness had forced everyone into hard-line positions. The board, with its clumsy "decision-making process" by which it was moved to act only when forced by pressure and threats had created an atmosphere of such mistrust that, even when its decisions produced some benefits, one faction or another inevitably believed a malign purpose lurked behind them. The disinterest of officials had left people without an outlet for constructive action; it was futile to try to deal with an inaccessible superintendent or a perplexed board president. Instead, people were left with no one to fight but one another. Students black and white,

parents black and white, and teachers black and white formed
their own groups to protect their interests as best they could.
The official structure had succeeded in one vital sense—the
only issue in Paterson on which there was agreement became
yet another means of dividing and weakening the public.

Nothing articulated this split better than the immediate
goals of the black and the white parents. The blacks wanted
a hot-lunch program. Except for the two high schools, all
schools in Paterson were closed during lunch, and mothers
had to stay home to prepare a meal or pay for a coffeeshop
lunch. In practice, large numbers of minority children ate
no lunches and, even if the mother packed a lunch, the child
was not permitted to stay in the building to eat it. The black
community had first proposed hot lunches four years before,
not free lunches, but the low-cost federal lunches supplied
by the majority of schools in the nation. Since their initial
request, they had received only promises, stalls, and rejec-
tions. That federal school lunches should have been considered anything but a reasonable request seems absurd, but in
the atmosphere of mistrust the white citizens could not regard
it as reasonable.

The most sinister plot that many whites thought the
board capable of initiating was busing. Although no civil-
rights leader in the city had suggested busing to end de facto
segregation and the board itself viewed the subject in horri-
fied silence, parents still saw the specter of busing everywhere.
They regarded the fact that children had to walk home for
lunch as built-in protection against this eventuality. The
board, as usual, had exacerbated their fears by keeping the
controversial consultant's report under wraps for several
months while rumors circulated about its contents. Rooney
accused the board of not holding its long-promised meeting
on the report because it was afraid to face the Taxpayers
Association's opposition. "They do things little by little," he

warned his followers, "and I caution you that implementing hot lunches throughout the city is another part of putting the busing program into effect."

Rooney seized on Paterson's large number of so-called affidavit pupils * as further proof of the plan to start busing. No one could convince him that state law required the city to educate these children. "I'd like to see us send 2,000 of our children over to Clifton and put them in their schools," he objected. "They'd send them right back. The real reason these children are here is that the politicians want them here. They're busing now to relieve this overcrowding and they'd like to bus more because there's a lot of money in bus contracts." "The politicians" were capable of almost anything, but to think that they wanted an extra 2,000 deprived kids in the schools was proof, not of a plot, but of the wretched fears the board's silence encouraged. Fear, nevertheless, was as powerful an organizing factor as anger, and the board had let both grow, until, ironically, it did not dare move in the face of the outrage it had helped to create.

On December 5, board Vice-President Jerome Levine stunned his fellow commissioners by announcing that he was quitting as head of the lunch-planning committee. "The board is not committed to the program," he said. "The feeling I've gotten is that people think, 'If we give them lunches, the next thing they'll be asking for breakfast.' This board won't vote against lunches," he concluded, "but it won't vote for them either."

---

* According to state law, the city had to educate "bona fide guests" of local residents. These affidavit pupils, mostly children from the South and Puerto Rico who had been sent to live with relatives or friends in the city for one reason or another, constituted a staggering ten percent of the Paterson school population, a figure which gives a grave indication of the family dissolution in the minority community. These children were resented as a serious financial drain because their parents paid no taxes in the city and many of them, living without parental supervision, were severely disturbed and troublesome.

Bessie Jamieson stood up immediately. The ice of restrained fury edged her voice. She was in an awkward position. Just a few days before, she had quieted her people, who wanted to take further action against the board by reminding them she had received a firm commitment to start the lunches. "The Federation will take this as an absolute slap in the face," she pronounced. "Never, at no time, did we agree to just a study of the lunch program. We've been studied enough." She demanded that the board vote immediately on its intentions. Mrs. Rauschenbach replied that it was impossible to vote because the lunches were not on the evening's official agenda and quickly moved to other matters. No other commissioner made a comment. A few days later Mrs. Rauschenbach issued an official statement, adamantly denying that the lunch plan was dead and pointing out it had merely been delayed by practical obstacles such as building a cafeteria. Her statement came too late, for no more than the whites believed their children would not be bused did the blacks believe their children would receive the lunches.

Action concerning the schools spilled over from board meetings to anxious meetings of parents, community groups, and finally, as was inevitable, exploded among the students themselves. The first shock came in January, when a group *1968* of dropouts attacked four students outside Eastside High School, injuring two of them seriously enough to require hospitalization. The attack would have been considered an everyday occurrence in a major city, but it made front-page news for days in Paterson. Although the assault had taken place outside the school, the next day Kramer ordered police from the Youth Guidance Bureau to start patrolling inside the building.

Eastside High School was seething. Built on top of a cemetery in 1927 and meant to hold 1,300 pupils, it now had

2,100, 46% black, 39% white, and 15% Spanish. Kennedy High had a similar ethnic makeup; it also had a bright, new building and vastly different administrative and educational policies. Eastside was run on a rigid "track" system, with all grades divided into classes for bright, average, and slow learners, while Kennedy had more flexibility and experimental programming. The situation of the board's running the two high schools on radically different premises resulted from the fact that Kennedy was newly administered while Eastside was still being run by decisions made decades ago. The black students charged that the "track" system was simply a device to segregate them within the building, but the board had declined to change the track system or even take the simple step of equalizing Eastside and Kennedy. The school's principal, who had already announced plans to retire at the end of the year, went on sick leave immediately following the attack, but the board did not use this opening to change the school.

Instead, the single solution offered by both the mayor and the board was to place guards inside the school building, a solution that made neither whites nor blacks comfortable. "School guards, policemen, whatever you want to call them, have no place inside any public school in the United States," declared the president of the teachers' union. (The fact that it is now necessary to have them in hundreds of schools does not change the value of this premise.) For the blacks the guards constituted the last straw. Their anger was perhaps out of proportion to the fact that there were only four policemen in Eastside, but the situation had become a vicious and visible symbol of the blacks' position in the city. In their view, the administration claimed not to have money to feed their children, but it did have the resources to treat them like criminals. They saw the guards as a deliberate attempt to implicate all young people in the actions of a few dropouts.

The mayor apparently had not noticed the mounting anger. "Every cuckoo clock in the world is coming to Paterson," he noted privately, referring to the outside troublemakers who had been attracted to Eastside by the publicity surrounding the attack. Publicly, however, he made no effort to dispel the general impression that the guards' sole purpose was to bear down on black students. Although P.T.A.'s in white areas would only have to voice their fears of busing to receive a personal visit and reassurance from the mayor, he refused to discuss Eastside with any delegation from the black community.

The black students at Eastside, in response, formed the Black Students Organization, whose primary objective was the guards' removal. The B.S.O. also formulated plans for revamping the school, including an end to the track system, an investigation of the guidance bureau, hanging pictures of black heroes in the halls, keeping the bathrooms supplied with toilet paper, and permission to fly an Afro-American flag. The students' optimism was striking. Adult militants urged them to back up their demands with action, but initially they rejected this approach and proceeded carefully through proper channels. They seemed to think that the situation had resulted from misunderstanding and that once officials in charge understood conditions at the school, changes would follow. They presented their demands first to the school administration, which told them they had to bring the matter to the attention of the board, and then twice to the board, where Mrs. Rauschenbach told them the "proper approach" was to speak to the school administration.

The black adults, meanwhile, pressed for a black administrator. Although Eastside's population was over one-half minority, they asked only that one of the two vice-principals be black. The board's next meeting was the most crowded of that year. Hundreds of people jammed the board room, sat on the floors, and spilled out into the corridors. Not one objection was made to the board's naming then vice-principal Jacob Weber to fill the principalship. Filling the vice-principalship, however, provoked hours of speeches. The blacks insisted that their request was just and education-ally sound. Their candidate, a teacher in the school, was known in the community as "a strict disciplinarian" and had the respect of the students. The blacks thought he could bring order and progress to the school. He needed two more courses, which he was taking over the summer, to complete certification for the post. "The board should only make this appointment if it insists upon forgetting all qualifications," declared Sokalski. The board, which had often appointed whites to positions temporarily under the same circumstances, refused to consider the black community's candidate or even the one black in the city who possessed certification; instead, it named a white administrator who later collapsed under the strain of his new post.

This action brought the board its bitterest condemnation of the year. The decision not only placed the black parents in the worst position possible—that of publicly failing their children—but terrified them for fear of what action the students would take in the face of this final provocation. They could hardly believe that the board members under-stood the full implications of their act and urgently tried to make them understand. Mrs. Natalie Riley, the gracious, middle-aged president of the Coordinating Council of Negro Women, stood up. "Reconsider your resolution or you'll live to regret it," she warned. "If you don't do this, Paterson will be afire. Please believe me." Her remarks, made in desper-ation, were taken by the board as a threat. "Once those kids get fed up and they look around, they're going to cut loose and no one will be able to stop them," another man warned. Mickey Levine, a junior at the school and son of the board vice-president, reflected the feeling of all the students—that the official proceedings no longer had anything to do with education: "The school is troubled by an administration that is more and more running scared, that is, depending on the police to solve its problems. If you don't come to your senses, I hope you are prepared to deal with the monster you are creating."

The board did not reconsider its resolution. The meeting had lasted several hours. The air in the room was almost unbreathable, filled with sweat, smoke, and despair, and over it hung Mrs. Riley's words: "You'll live to regret it."

We are all sympathetic with the police and their problems. But the very existence of government as a useful social device is threatened if it does not bring to justice those persons who under cover of governmental authority act unlawfully in terrorizing citizens. I therefore charge you to investigate this matter vigorously with a view of leaving no means unused in ascertaining the identity of the individual police officers who engaged in and who bear responsibility for the acts of criminal misconduct during the first week of July.

—JOHN CRANE
Passaic County Assignment Judge

Sergeant Peter Le Conte has a classic sergeant's time-worn face, a petite strawberry-blonde wife, a son who served in Vietnam, and a suburban home with a swimming pool that he built himself. He is the city's "top cop," its most decorated officer. He has been on the force for twenty-eight years and of him Police Commissioner Edwin Englehardt says, "I can honestly say he is one cop who stands out like a shining star." Short, squarely built, with thick, dark hair, he is known on the force as "the immortal sergeant" and in the ghetto by a variety of quite different names. He has the added distinction of being the only policeman in Paterson who has been indicted twice; he was found innocent in both instances.

Le Conte's designation as being the most indicted and most decorated police officer may have been ironic, but it was no accident. It does not simply reflect Paterson's individual caprices, but typifies the anomalous state of police science throughout the United States. The Graham Avenue attack, like police scandals in other cities, brought into glaring focus the problems which had been eating away at the department for years. Between November and December 1968, in the wake of the attack nearly five percent of the Paterson police force was indicted or fired on charges ranging from misconduct in office to complicity in a burglary ring. The series of indictments had a sensational effect on the city. Officials tended to write off each incident as an exception, stating that "good, hardworking, sincere, dedicated" officers made up the majority of the department. However, since these weren't the ones causing the trouble, this answer proved unsatisfactory.

If the schools were under "control" in the sense that they were dominated by political influences, the police in Paterson and other cities represented an institution that was no longer under control for any purpose. Their complete autonomy from the public—which has been a striking feature of many American urban police departments and a decisive factor behind corruption, brutality, and other problems—has originated from a combination of sources. The social conflicts in American cities have consistently produced such violence and tension that the police, needed as they have been for peace-keeping and protection, early obtained a relatively exclusive position in urban society (de Tocqueville's "armed force" always at the ready). Moreover, where the people have little influence over their government as a whole, the law-enforcement machinery—the ultimate weapon of government—will be the last institution they will control. Paterson's police force has traditionally been the tool of the city's rulers, whether industrialists or politicians, rather than an organic part of the community.

The protected status of the police also results from the fact that urban residents have not cared to question police behavior. As the centers for "illegal" businesses, for example, the cities have been content to come to a tacit understanding with their police departments, allowing them to go their own way: very few people in Paterson wanted to see liquor laws enforced during Prohibition and few are interested in seeing gambling laws enforced now. More important, since the cities have been left to cope with the problems and failures of an entire society, this has meant in practice that the urban police have been left to contend with these problems. In a society which cares so little how its cities as a whole function, the police methods for contending with its failures are hardly a matter for public scrutiny. In Paterson, as elsewhere, about seventy-five percent of the calls to the police have nothing to do with law enforcement or the job for which the men have been trained, but concern social problems (family disputes), housing (no heat), education (truancy, school guards), and so on.

The Paterson police had inherited a difficult legacy at best, but complicating it further was Graves' six years of making law enforcement the focus of his administration. On the surface Graves' constant attention gave Paterson perhaps the most tightly run force in the country. He instinctively understood that peculiar combination of discipline and brute excitement which characterizes the business of being a policeman. He propelled the department into spit-and-polish condition; he assigned, promoted, and chastised the men, stopped his car to rush out and correct their traffic-directing techniques, and sometimes dropped by the Detective Bureau to help question prisoners. He also invested their relatively dirty jobs with a sense of glamour. He instituted the use of a code-number system over the police radio, adding a touch of snappy professionalism, and his policy of answering all police calls within ninety seconds saw the men on constant alert, racing their cars with sirens wailing through the streets. (Kramer immediately abandoned this policy, charging that it had caused a twenty-eight percent increase in squad-car collisions.)

Beneath this surface discipline, however, was a department that a consultant to Governor Hughes' Commission on Civil Disorders later described as being the worst in the state, certainly worse than Newark's and possibly the worst in the country. The combination of consistent glory and unqualified protection from City Hall was a heady one for the police as more and more the department responded solely to the wishes of one man. The department became so absorbed in publicity-seeking projects, such as raids and roundups, that it paid little attention to the basic patrolling and investigating functions that provide protection for the public. Men often solved cases simply by marking them "cleared" in the official records. Although drug-related crime constituted the city's worst police problem, there was only one man in the Narcotics Bureau. The top-heavy command structure, under which Paterson had an extraordinary supervisor-to-patrolman ratio of 1 to 2.4 compared to a normal ratio of 1 to 8, made few men available to pursue the basic but unglamourous duties.

Paterson's police had attained a more protected position than is common in most American cities, and such a marked interference in the city's life that one prominent City Hall employee described Paterson simply as "a police state." The police seemed to be everywhere, all-powerful, and much to be feared. Graves approved personally the roster of men assigned to protect the polls on election days. A later study by the International Association of Chiefs of Police blamed the top-heavy command structure on promotions' having been made "on a wholesale basis as a method for repaying friendships or for political reasons" and cited "improper interference" in police operations. Charges of brutality were frequent. In 1964 the state ordered Passaic County to convene a grand jury to investigate reports that the Paterson police had tortured one prisoner by burning his body with matches and pouring alcohol down his nose. The grand jury made no indictments but handed down the rather unusual recommendation that the department photograph prisoners both before and after questioning.

There was one essential fact that Graves understood about the police—men who carry guns and engage in a job as brutal as it is brutalizing must be kept under tight command. Its defects were myriad, but the department would not undertake any major action without the approval of the civilian authority represented by the mayor. Graves repeatedly charged that the July 3 attack would never have occurred while he was in office. "I had them on a leash," he explained. "They're used to being kept on a leash and Kramer let them go. What do you expect would happen?"

"We lost our leader and no one has taken his place," a detective commented. "We hated him while he was here, but without him, we're floundering." Having no brake, this department, accustomed to regarding itself as above the law and to enforcing its will viciously, fell into anarchy.

Kramer had never remotely considered that the police would become a major area of contention in an administration which had so optimistically promised to concentrate its efforts on physically rebuilding the city. Like most civilians, he had succumbed to the "police mystique" and was convinced that the work, with its quasi-military mannerisms and aura of casual violence, was outside his administrative powers. During the campaign he had released a "white paper," proposing to reform the department by depoliticizing it and "giving it back to the professionals"—meaning the police themselves. In office, against considerable evidence to the contrary, he clung to the belief that the police would "clean their own house" partly because it was his idealized concept of how a city agency should run and partly because he was wary of them.

Despite his apprehension, Kramer recognized that change was necessary and, in an effort to protect himself from the department's antagonism and Graves' constant charges that he was destroying the police, sought his solution through "the professional approach." He hired the International Association of Chiefs of Police, a consultant group based in Washington, D.C., to study the department and make recommendations for restructuring it. The $25,000 report by the "best police study group in the United States," as Kramer described the I.A.C.P., was slated to take six months, but was not finished when promised. The complete breakdown of the department occurred before it appeared, and it was not until nearly two years after he took office, and several months after the July 3 attack, that Kramer began to move with the police.

Kramer later stated that one of the worst mistakes of his administration was having left the police alone. "I backed off when I got my fingers burned," he commented. "Well, I shouldn't have." But he was not the only mayor in the United States sitting on top of a police department that was brutal, mismanaged, and corrupt. Mayors who have done well in other categories have recoiled from the political and emotional consequences of confronting the police. In Paterson the combination of extreme police insularity and a public long accustomed to regarding "strong" law enforcement as the single method of getting the job done, made the situation particularly difficult. "The only real solution to that department," one police reporter felt, "was clearing out half the men and starting all over again." In view of the circumstances and the department's condition, Kramer's later efforts did produce marked, if hardly thorough, improvements.

But those later efforts did not provide the city any satisfaction in the aftermath of the raid, which, as a subsequent grand jury presentment emphasized, demanded immediate action from the mayor. The raid had been so shocking that even those groups who had no interest in seeing the men involved punished began to realize that the chaotic department could not provide consistent professional protection for the public. But the mayor's office answered neither the burning question of punishment nor the pervasive question of restructuring the force. Instead, Kramer persisted in waiting for the I.A.C.P. study, which he felt would give him the firm backing he needed to proceed. And while he waited, the department continued to deteriorate as the hysteria over law and order in Paterson continued to mount.

The Police and Fire Board bore the primary responsibility for police conduct. The four-member board included what the newspapers like to call "Paterson's three most eligible bachelors": Robert Shavick, the chairman; Edwin Englehardt, the police commissioner; and Ken Hayden, who was not a voting member, but the clerk of the board. The board also represented an astounding complex of political alliances and the animosity between its members, as well as their conflicting loyalties, virtually assured that the board would flounder in performing its public duties.

Shavick, a wealthy, handsome lawyer, was originally a Graves' appointee, who had no personal ambitions and did not obstruct Kramer. He conducted the board's meetings with a kind of biting, elegant humor and, possessing an acute sense of order, kept the board from erupting into verbal brawls or settling into tedious wrangling. However, the board's dealings with the police department itself were not so precise; and the civil-rights' groups, not satisfied with bemused decorum as a substitute for responsibility, later initiated a lawsuit against Shavick.

Edwin Englehardt, the police commissioner, possessed the unique ability to swim through shifting currents with more aplomb than Sam Patch had ever shown. An unpretentious-looking man who wore his hair slicked back in a ducktail, Englehardt had long been one of Graves' closest associates as well as his business partner. Since Englehardt was technically a Republican, Graves had appointed him to the board to satisfy the legal requirement that it have equal membership from both parties. Englehardt also owned a hardware store which was a major local supplier to the board of education. When Kramer took office, the police commissioner became one of the first of the former mayor's sidekicks to turn his allegiance to the new mayor. Before Kramer, it had been universally presumed that running as a Republican for the Paterson mayoralty was, as Kramer once said, "like taking a ride on the *Titanic*." The thought that he could be next intrigued Englehardt. (His store also continued selling supplies to the board of education during Kramer's administration, $190,000 worth in the 1968–69 school year alone.)

Englehardt took the most active role among the board members. He vociferously defended law and order, and consistently voted against firing policemen accused of charges ranging from brutality to misconduct. Although he possessed no professional background in law enforcement and the board, by statute, was only a policy-making body, he constantly interfered with police operations. At one point, Englehardt even took a well-publicized trip to Washington, where he sought a personal appointment with J. Edgar Hoover (which he did not receive) with the object of asking the F.B.I. director why the bureau was "spending so much time investigating the police in Paterson and so little time investigating agitators." Although neither the F.B.I. nor state and county investigations had developed any evidence to support this notion, he was convinced that agitators from the Fourth Ward had contrived to set off the Spanish riot. And he did not believe in brutality. "You'll find," he contended, "that when any member of a minority group is arrested, a charge of brutality is almost automatically filed. That way they think they're going to scare the police into overlooking' certain acts. But, thank God, the men on our force are dedicated professionals. The people of this town really depend on their police. The mayor knows that, the department knows that." He described it as "a young, progressive department," which was "craving for minority members," constantly seeking new methods "to keep on top of the spiraling crime rate," and "doing everything possible to reach out to the community." This was the same department, without one minority member above the rank of patrolman, that often solved cases by marking them "cleared," and that helped to sabotage Kramer's community-relations program.

Conrad Corsini, an elderly Italian, was the hard-line commissioner on the board. A lifelong Democrat and friend of Graves, he also had a streak of stubborn independence. He had astounded the city by endorsing Kramer. With his close-cropped white hair, full pink cheeks, and the bow tie that he customarily wore framing his face, Corsini looked like a benign cherub. He did not, however, feel benign. In his view, honesty and an absolute emphasis on law enforcement were the only two things that could save the city. Convinced that Kramer was promoting open rebellion through his "soft" positions, he had quickly pulled away from the young mayor. But Corsini reserved his special wrath for Englehardt. Englehardt, to some extent, supported Kramer's efforts to change the department. Corsini, however, regarded the whole matter as a political ploy, the police commissioner as a man who was selling out "Paterson's finest," and demanded a full-scale probe of Englehardt's "political influence" in the department. Corsini could barely stay in Englehardt's presence without denouncing him and few meetings ended without mutual accusations that they were liars, prejudiced (against Italians), politically motivated, and self-serving.

In addition to its internal disagreements, the Police and Fire Board had lost all concept of being a legitimate civilian watchdog on the police. In the wake of the raid, it not only took no action regarding the police misconduct, but it declined outright to start an investigation. Kramer supported this decision. "I called in the F.B.I. immediately," he said in his defense. "You have to remember that they were very involved in civil rights then and I felt they were the people with the expertise to handle it best. If the board had held hearings at that point, it would have polarized the whole city. Can you imagine, in that tense atmosphere, the charges and countercharges inflaming everyone day after day? I just couldn't do it. It would have hurt the city more than it would have helped. In any case," he noted in a perhaps unintentional evaluation of the board's membership, "nobody would have believed them no matter what they found. One half of the city would have accused them of a whitewash and the other half of injuring the department."

By a predictable turn of fate, the board's equivocation produced worse consequences than would have resulted from a momentary uproar. The July 3 raid simply was not an event that would disappear into the obscure recesses of the F.B.I. It had seared the city, and because it was not settled rapidly, it developed into an issue that continued to upset every faction in Paterson even years later. The board's indifference out-

202 □ □ □

raged the blacks perhaps more than the raid itself had; they pressed the matter until the county, state, and federal governments all initiated lengthy grand jury probes that eventually produced such bizarre highlights that the *National Enquirer* took note of the proceedings. As a result of this constant turmoil, many whites and conservative groups were outraged. Many who had not yet been offered convincing public proof of those moments of terror and unprovoked assault along Graham Avenue could not believe that the Paterson police were capable of such an action. The anger of the blacks mystified them, just as the ensuing probes by "outsiders" such as the F.B.I. agents, deputy state attorneys general, and Justice Department representatives irritated them. And most particularly the city resented having its failures become a focus of national publicity, its police department attacked on television, and its own life constant fare for critical headlines.

As for the police department itself, for the three years following the raid it became the single most probed, investigated, and studied department in the nation. The entire force was tainted by the actions of a few and its demoralization was complete.

The first investigation started a week after the July 3 raid. Following the city's refusal to take action, the blacks looked to the county prosecutor's office; Thevos did not volunteer for duty. Civil-rights groups, led by the Southern Christian Leadership Conference, appealed to Governor Hughes, who personally ordered Thevos to "hear the complaints of the community." Consequently, Thevos had to undertake the formality of empaneling a grand jury. This action by itself, however, meant little, for the prosecutor's office presents—in confidence—the evidence which convinces a grand jury whether or not to indict individuals. Thevos assigned one assistant prosecutor to the case, who worked on it with unexpected diligence, but because of the confusion of events and with some 300 potential witnesses, a full staff of investigators would have been required to sort out accounts. Moreover, the tape recorder at headquarters which automatically recorded orders to the men in the field had mysteriously broken down that night, making it difficult to ascertain the whereabouts of individual officers.

The S.C.L.C. members undertook the responsibilities of paid public officials—rounding up witnesses, finding translators to aid Spanish complaints, forcing the police department to issue "a mug book" containing pictures of all the men on the force for identification—and finally, over the objections of the prosecutor's office, the S.C.L.C. also managed to obtain "police line-ups." As many as eighty officers a day were called to court to be viewed by witnesses. The mug book and line-ups constituted such a stunning role reversal that they made national news. The spectacle of the entire force's being treated like common criminals swamped police morale and inflamed public opinion.

On October 8 the Passaic County Grand Jury completed its three-month investigation and handed down a presentment * of its findings. Considering that the twenty-three-member grand jury included a majority of middle-aged, white suburbanites and only one black, the fact that it confirmed every charge made against the Paterson police was particularly striking. "There was irrefutable evidence presented to this grand jury," the presentment began, "that in the early-morning hours of July 3, certain members of the Paterson Police Department arrived in police vehicles in the Graham Avenue area, a predominately black neighborhood, and deliberately broke the windows of several stores owned by black

---

* A presentment is a report that describes illegal actions without actually fixing blame by indicting individuals.

shopkeepers. This was attested by a number of eyewitnesses, some of whom could be termed unimpeachable." Similarly damaging testimony showed that carloads of police arrived at the S.C.L.C., threw tear-gas bombs inside, and departed. Testimony also indicated the use of police tactics "repulsive to every concept of proper police behavior." These included "the so-called 'goon-squad' tactic of selecting an individual from the street and administering a vicious beating to him at some isolated location, leaving the victim there as an example to others." The grand jury also noted that the police, especially superior officers, had not notably cooperated with the investigation. "The attitude expressed was that they felt the alleged incidents at the S.C.L.C. headquarters and Graham Avenue were inconceivable and therefore probably did not happen." The jurors said other testimony "cast doubt" upon this "widespread professed ignorance."

Only two sections of the long and revealing report, however, held vital interest for city officials and the Police and Fire Board. One explained the difficult situation the police faced: "At times, they were but a thin, blue line separating a force, in which some elements openly threatened to level portions of the city, from that accomplishment. In most cases the Paterson Police Department performed its difficult assignment in a commendable manner." This became the most quoted phrase in the presentment, as the administration constantly pointed out that "even the grand jury said the police performed commendably." The second section was mentioned less frequently: "At the time the allegations were advanced, it was incumbent upon the department, its supervisory board, and the City itself to forthwith investigate the charges. In the face of this, for the Police and Fire Board Commissioners . . . to fail to even convene a meeting to discuss what should or might be done . . . was tantamount to that Board abdicating its responsibility over the Paterson

Police Department. Nor was this inaction excusable by reason of the concurrence therein by the highest city official and the police department itself." This last observation opened city officials to the possibility of legal action for neglect of duty.

In the face of this "irrefutable evidence," the absence of indictments was remarkable. Judge Crane, head of the Passaic County court system, placed the grand jury under extraordinary instructions and ordered it to continue sitting until it came up with indictments or exhausted itself. The S.C.L.C. went still further and filed a civil suit naming the state attorney general and the county prosecutor as defendants. It accused Thevos of purposely glossing over the probe; the suit also contended that as long as the probe remained in local hands, it would never be conducted properly and witnesses would be too terrified to come forward. (The grand jury had noted that many witnesses were "unable or unwilling" to identify their alleged attackers.) The S.C.L.C. asked the court to order the state attorney to take over the investigation of the police.

This role reversal was breathtaking. The S.C.L.C. now had the officials who had ignored the blacks' demands for justice sitting in court, however tenuously. After fighting the case for two months, Thevos finally came to the realization that it would in fact be easier for him to let the state contend with the explosive police probe and personally asked the state attorney general to assign a special prosecutor to the case. In December a state attorney general took over, a new grand jury was later empaneled, and the months-long process of investigating "the early-morning hours of July 3" started once again.

Meanwhile, the persistent attempt of the blacks to gain justice through legal, "proper" channels brought them no plaudits. Going to court had offered none of the exhilaration and excitement of sit-ins; it involved months of drudgery, of seeing subpoenas served, motions filed, and witnesses brought forward. But those who felt that the police probes were destroying Paterson and those who knew that the truth, if ever found, would destroy them condemned it equally. Monsignor Wall, the stalwart, conservative fighter against corruption, denounced the grand juries as the tools of "the do-gooders and appeasers." The state P.B.A. issued constant expressions of outrage. Death threats poured in against S.C.L.C. members.

Yet these cases represented a quiet, but rather remarkable tribute to the city. A steadfast courage somehow endured among the ordinary, anonymous citizens of Paterson. Junius Sturdifen, an elderly barber, gave an idea of the terror of people caught between rioters and rioting policemen. "To us, it was the acme of absurdity that police officers were being accused of these acts," he testified. "Now we didn't know where to turn. It was my feeling that without some positive action immediately, the whole town would go up. Then the message go through the grapevine: Maybe if you saw this, it's best not to say. If you want to live, it's best not to say this." Yet the city's legacy, the dream which had brought group after group to its tenements, had persisted. That many people who knew it was "best not to" did testify, was a monument to the deep faith in justice and belief in vindication under the American system that Paterson was still able to summon up.

In the confusion of probes and countersuits, the fact that the Paterson Police Department also showed minimal competence in its job of fighting crime had temporarily faded into the background. Like many urban departments, the Paterson department had been able to ride along on the law-and-order issue; crime was its defense, not its motivation. The probes also provoked the attendant question of how the raid had occurred in the first place. Once attention had been focused on the department, its faults could not escape becoming a serious public issue.*

The raid and ensuing scandals brought the leadership of the Paterson Police Department under close scrutiny. The official chief, John O'Brien, was seriously ill and often hospitalized. In his absence, Deputy Chief Angelo Esposito effectively took charge. Esposito, a man who held himself with ramrod straightness and spoke little, was Graves' protégé; and he had risen from sergeant to deputy chief during the former mayor's tenure. Holding a fervent view of law and order, he thought that a firm show of force constituted the best defense against anarchy. Asked how the raid had occurred without his knowledge, after being summoned to the grand jury, Esposito told reporters that the first he had heard about it was the following morning, when Chief O'Brien asked him if he knew anything about what had happened on Graham Avenue. This answer did not satisfy everyone in Paterson. When the police mug book was issued for witnesses to identify their alleged attackers, Esposito immediately announced that the department would file criminal charges against any person who made an identification of a police officer that was not later upheld in court. (This was not legally possible. Criminal charges could only be placed if witnesses had conspired together to make false identifications.)

* Aside from its inefficiency, there was also a question of exactly how corrupt the Paterson department was. However, the answer to that question did not even begin to be answered until 1973, when the state attorney general's offices started scrutinizing the Paterson police. The probe, which is incomplete as of this writing, centers on an array of activities, including alleged ties between some members of the Paterson police, the prosecutor's office, the judiciary, and organized crime for possible involvement in a sentence-fixing scheme for convicted criminals. The probe is further delving into the possible involvement of certain Paterson policemen in narcotics traffic, gambling, and perhaps murder. State law-enforcement officials said they expected the probe "could lead to big people."

Despite the mounting discontent with the department, as the city's one deputy chief and the only man eligible to take over for O'Brien, Esposito continued to sit as Paterson's head law-enforcement officer for several months after the raid. Esposito was very popular in some circles, which partly accounted for Kramer's reluctance to remove him. Kramer also left Esposito in command because he hadn't much choice. After the position of mayor, the job of police chief may be the most difficult in a city. It requires a man who possesses the rare combination of a military mind edged with sensitivity, capable of imposing the tough discipline necessary to direct the force and deal with the tense, delicate realities of city life. Esposito undoubtedly had the military mind. Moreover, finding new leadership in a department where Graves' followers held most command positions would not be easy.

Nevertheless, it seems that Esposito's political beliefs as well as his actions contributed to his downfall. Kramer decided to keep him on as the next chief, if he would modify his hard-line position. In view of the intense opposition to Esposito in some sectors of the city, the mayor did not relay this offer openly, but secretly through key administration officials. The chiefship was the prize of Esposito's world. Yet ironically he turned out to be one of the few officials in the city who wasn't willing to bend for his own advancement. He had "his principles," he said, and the deputy chief with the ramrod back and salt-and-pepper hair "told them what they could do with their chiefship," as he put it long afterward.

Kramer finally settled on an obscure captain who seemed capable of running the force and prepared to raise him in rank. On September 30, nearly three months after the raid, the Police and Fire Board met in a secret session, which the press discovered by accident, marking Kramer's first move to assert command of the police. Over Corsini's furious objections, the board introduced an ordinance creating two new deputy-chief posts, finally opening the door to displacing Esposito from his clear succession. Kramer had hoped to avoid controversy, but public confidence was so low that nothing could have brought more attention than this furtive method of dealing with Esposito. Corsini loudly declared it "a new low in dirty politics."

Kramer's indirect approach also had adverse effects within the department itself. The administration had seriously failed those officers who were attempting to do their jobs and whose position had become untenable both publicly and professionally. Lieutenant Anthony Ignoffo, for example, had headed the Narcotics Bureau for ten years. He had hardly enjoyed Graves' administration, but had lost any hope that the department would change under Kramer and, fed up with the frustrations of his post, he resigned. Other men were sickened by the hostility they had to bear because of the actions of a few. "During the riot, they had me directing traffic," commented one patrolman. "There were about 500 people standing around, catcalling and sometimes throwing bottles. I tell you, if anyone of them had come near me, I don't know what I would have done with him. And, you know, it probably would have been an innocent one, too. Sure, there's some guys who shouldn't be on the force and they've made things worse. But we're not all like that."

Further, by not disciplining transgressors, the Paterson department had created a dangerous situation where some men had decided their badges constituted permission to take part in a free-for-all. After the raid in July, the next major incident, when two patrolmen falsely claimed that some black teenagers had shot at them, occurred in August, causing another citywide controversy. In November a burglary ring was exposed, after which three officers were indicted. There were more men under suspicion, but the department did not have enough evidence to bring charges. One of these men was also indicted for inducing a civilian to steal for him in another case and, finally, for trying to bribe the outcome of his own trial, thus attaining a new department record. "That's just what we need, another police scandal," Graves said in blaming the situation on Kramer.

A few weeks after the burglary ring's exposure, the I.A.C.P. study, the ammunition that Kramer had been cautiously waiting for, finally became public. In unrelenting detail it documented the department's total failure in technical and human terms: The department lacked a clear-cut command structure, adequate record keeping or communications, and its training was below par. It was viciously divided by political infighting. It should take immediate and extensive steps to improve its community relations. Graves was not mentioned by name in the report, but it placed most of the blame on "past administrations."

Kramer finally moved and made public recognition of the radical measures needed. The next day he made a terse and surprising announcement: "I know we have highly qualified policemen in top positions, but they have lived under the heavy hand of political alignment for too many years, and I am most fearful that they will be hampered in the unbiased and impartial implementation of the report without regard to factionalism. Consequently, I am by virtue of the authority invested in me as Chief Executive, moving to hire the finest professional policemen available in the United States today to take charge of our department for one year and supervise its restructuring. And I will expect complete and total cooperation at all levels."

Cooperation was exactly what the mayor did not receive. The idea of bringing in an outsider appalled many people in Paterson, who already blamed outsiders like the grand jury and F.B.I. for tampering with the department.

An imported "superchief" struck some as being the kiss of death. Graves blasted the I.A.C.P. report. "When a big outfit like that comes in, of course they have to say a lot of spectacular things just to show they've earned their money." The report, he stated, was "a political trick," "a waste of taxpayers' money," and any problems in the police department could be solved by "the mayor of this city sitting down and cracking some heads together."

The days turned colder. It was now nearly five months since the emotions playing like fire across the face of America had erupted twice in Paterson on hot July nights. Those nights were burned on the city's heart, but nothing had since changed in the area along Main Street where it had started. The boards were still nailed to broken windows, and shopkeepers, their insurance canceled, wouldn't undertake the expense of putting in new glass. Evidence that the federal government had noticed the area was confined to the two articles that had been there before the riot—one portable swimming pool, left over from the summer recreation program, and the looming, abrupt end of Route 80. Evidence that New Jersey had noticed this patch of the Garden State was confined to its ten-percent portion of Route 80. The county's only visible interest was a new courthouse under construction—a square, windowless building. The bar association had insisted that it have no windows, presumably to keep street noises from interfering with the administration of justice, but more likely because the street scene had become so ugly that no one wanted to be reminded of it.

Yet it was to that windowless building, or more precisely, the old courthouse alongside the incomplete new structure, to which all Paterson looked to find the results of those July nights. The question was simply who would be punished and who would not. The courts had already dealt with over 100 defendants arrested during the riot, but no policeman had yet been indicted.

On November 22, Commissioner Englehardt was drinking his morning coffee at an auxiliary firehouse also used to hold classes for police trainees. Englehardt was waiting for WXTV to do a special report on the recently started Spanish language and culture classes for the police that made Paterson's the only department in the state offering its recruits such a program. Englehardt read the *News* as he waited. The first grand jury, the one Judge Crane had ordered to stay in session until it came up with indictments or exhausted itself, had disbanded. "Do you see this? No indictments. That should settle it," Englehardt jubilantly declared. The police were in a high mood of relief and Sergeant Le Conte, who had been transferred from the Tactical Patrol Force to a less sensitive position in the training program, joked with the young men as the class got underway. Englehardt issued a formal statement saying the grand jury had "vindicated the department." But F.B.I agents kept bringing to a federal grand jury in Newark evidence from the kind of exhaustive investigation that had not been conducted locally.

A week before Christmas, the event occurred that one half the city had hoped for and the other half had feared. The federal grand jury indicted eight policemen on civil-rights charges stemming from the events of July 3. Although the civil-rights charges in the province of the federal government were light compared to the crimminal charges that the county or state could have found, the indictments came as a shock. In the publicity of the local probes, the federal investigation had been almost forgotten and practically every-one had concluded that, whether it deserved to be or not, the department would be vindicated. The indictments in-cluded three well-known figures: Sergeant Le Conte; Ser-geant Abe Hemsey, a former P.B.A. president who had worked closely with Graves; and Patrolman Joseph Grossi, Jr., a nephew of Tony Grossi.

Reactions were swift and fierce. Calls from people wanting to contribute to defense costs flooded police headquarters. Chief O'Brien condemned the indictments as "an outrage." The state P.B.A. president accused the grand jury of "playing footsies with the element," an accusation he did not explain more fully. Many in Paterson were still so unaware of the condition of the city's life that, despite "the irrefutable evidence" and the indictments, they found it difficult to believe that the unprovoked assault on Graham Avenue had taken place. Even the grand jurors, who after an intensive three months' study had more knowledge about the attack than any whites, did not seem to comprehend the nature of police power in Paterson. Witnesses were occasionally amazed by the jurors' naïveté. "Some of them kept asking us why, when this was happening, we didn't stop it," remarked one witness. "You know, like it was our duty as citizens to keep the police from doing things like that."

The only evidence that Paterson would have accepted was its own evidence, an acknowledgment from city officials, rather than from outsiders. This was not forthcoming. Kramer, who had often stated that "these men must be found for the good of the others and to restore the reputation of the department," seemed to have changed his mind in the face of furor. Every indicted policeman in the history of the city had been suspended on the theory that "the public must be protected from the appearance of wrong as well as actual wrongs"; Kramer immediately announced that the men would not be suspended "if I can help it.

Two days later the Police and Fire Board met for a crowded emergency session. Television crews from New York were in the mayor's office, at the S.C.L.C., and all over Paterson, recording this moment of reckoning. The expected deadlock occurred. Shavick and Hall voted for suspension; Corsini and Englehardt, against. The mayor was summoned from his office where the Lincoln quote hung next to his desk. He declared his belief in "the great American concept of innocent until proven guilty" and voted against suspension. Kramer's critics accused him of making a callous political decision, but it also seems doubtful that he would have decided differently under any circumstances; no mayor can afford to live in open warfare with the police. The meeting broke up in intense excitement as everyone rushed forward to give his opinion before the television cameras.

Privately some city officials were disturbed by the indictments for other reasons. "That grand jury really goofed," as one official put it. "They got some of the wrong guys." The eight policemen were arraigned at a federal district court in January 1969. Two years later their trials had not yet started, while the city and "some of the wrong guys" went through more years of pain and uncertainty for a matter that should have been settled in a few months.

The day after the board's meeting, Lieutenant Joseph Grossi, Sr., stood behind the booking desk near the entrance to police headquarters. Generally known in the city as "the nicest of the Grossi brothers," the lieutenant was the father of the indicted patrolman and the brother of the county Democratic chairman. The city had resumed its Christmas preparations. Inside the dimly-lit headquarters, Grossi's pleasant lined face fell in sadness. Years of raising a son and years of devotion to duty had crumbled in the single moment of the indictments. "Now, there's a boy as good as gold," he said quietly, "and look what's happened. Many of his superiors have come to me—they just came, I didn't ask them—and told me what a good boy he is. He only ever tried to do his job. He doesn't hate anybody. But you hear the things they say about him now."

Many people in Paterson, the majority in positions of public trust, knew for certain which policemen had been involved in "criminal misconduct" during the first week of July. They did not come forward. A black man left in a vacant lot with his head split open by a "goon squad," a policeman's "boy as good as gold"—all were equally sacrificed to political expediency.

Flesh behind steel and glass is unprotected
From enemies that whisper to the blood;
The scratch forgotten is the scratch infected;
The ruminant, reason, chews a poisoned cud.

—THEODORE ROETHKE
Prognosis *

Paterson approached the new year of 1969 a city close to collapse. The implacable forces of its structure and heritage clashed against aspirations for reform. Where the public did not have an effective hold on the municipal government, administration after administration had succumbed to the controlling powers. It was harshly clear to most people in Paterson that their intense effort to build an honest, responsive government had failed. In the face of the "irrefutable evidence" of wrongs, the next question became where were the city's residents to turn? The July 3 attack represented

* From *The Collected Poems of Theodore Roethke*. Copyright 1941 by Theodore Roethke. Reprinted by permission of Doubleday & Co., Inc.

the first and only time in the city's history that the county, state, and federal governments had all examined one aspect of Paterson's malfunctioning in view of the constitutional guarantees of a democratic society. Each level of government had conducted extensive investigations, some lasting for months, and altogether costing millions of dollars. Each had agreed that the law as well as the civil rights of citizens had been violated. In the end each did nothing. Clearly the federal, state, and county governments were not "useful social devices" which might have served Paterson. They never had been.

And, as always, this inability to get a response from the urban structure cost the city the very stability it needed so badly. Paterson, like many other cities, seemed to require its citizens either to leave or to surrender some part of their humanity if they stayed. Like the whites who had been unable to protect their neighborhoods, now the blacks, as the latest challenge to the city, experienced the same pressure to leave. Jeff Mallory, the vice-president of the Southern Christian Leadership Conference, was an example of a man who had held a vision of hope for the city; he had tried, failed, and finally surrendered his vision. As the chief architect behind the police probes, he became probably the most hated individual in Paterson. A tall, heavy-set man with an easygoing smile, years later he is still surprised by the threats, harassment, and intimidation that were directed at him. To Mallory the issue was clear. "This thing, the racism, the police behaving like that, it's like a cancer," he said. "You can see it growing. It has to be cut out or it will kill the town.

"The dues I paid for trying to build up my town and make it a clean, wholesome place to live was that I lost everything. . . . I lost my wife and family. She couldn't take it no more—the people calling up at all hours, threatening to kill her, kill the kids, the cars coming in the night and shining their lights on the house, yelling names from the street. . . . I couldn't put it together. I had my sheer knowledge of what had taken place from living through it and then there was what I had been taught to think about living in a democracy. It didn't make no sense. Never had I thought things like this would happen in the town where I was born and raised. . . . People ask me, 'Jeff, are you bitter?' " He shakes his head slowly. "I don't feel bitter. I don't feel nothing. You know the old story about the man without a country. That's what I feel like."

After January 1, 1969, in addition to its normal turmoil, the madness known as a mayoral campaign overtook the city. Paterson looked forward to the contest pitting the enterprising Kramer against the wily Graves. Many people were expecting the most fantastic election battle they would witness in their lifetimes. The stories of elections past, when the city had thrived on corruption charges by day and street brawls by night, were retold again and again. Let the newspapers write editorials about bad public manners! Paterson didn't really mind. Whatever else it had lost, the city would show that it still knew how to put on a mayoral election. The backroom boys laid in extra cigars, the bookies got out their tally sheets, and secret meetings occupied the nights of every person who held an official position or aspired to one. Ward leaders started the slow process of forays into the tenements and back streets; ideally they should know every voter in the district by sight. This tradition was hard to maintain, but some old-timers still managed, for in the great celebration of democracy, they defended everyone's right to vote—including the dead and the nonexistent.

This was to be no simple choice between right and wrong, honesty and corruption, the smiling young face against the old familiar one. Everyone understood that the forces of the old mayor had still ruled alongside the aspirations of the new mayor. Kramer's image had become very tarnished while the memory of Graves' worst excesses had faded. In the labyrinth of the city's life it was almost impossible to distinguish the final truth about either one. Was Kramer's concern "just a public relations gimmick," as a reporter said, or was he a dedicated man who, in the words of one supporter, had "held out against circumstances that would have taxed the patience of a Job"? Was Graves the "most arrogant mayor this city ever had," as an elderly ward leader charged, or simply what he himself expressed, "a man whose love for this city is equal to no other"?

Yet between them they symbolized a choice of historic proportions. To many it seemed impossible to "reform" the city without actually losing control of it to a dangerous degree. They had taken a timid step into the future with Kramer, found it terrifying, and longed for any semblance of order, even one as fierce as Graves' concept. (One vision of the future was ten miles down the road in, Newark, and that seemed a fate to avoid at any price.) Then there were those yearning to put the final touch to the past, to accept even Kramer's contradictions in order to prove once and for all that the city had some hope of freeing itself.

Kramer had not definitely made up his mind to run again. In January he took another of his frequent, mysterious trips to Washington, leading to speculation that he was seeking a post with the Republican national administration, which would permit him to bow out of Paterson with his dignity intact. Nevertheless, the realities of facing an election year and of knowing that the long underground battle would end one way or the other slowly put him into a better frame of mind. He might bow out or be defeated, but he would no longer have to suffer the embarrassment of being the chief executive of a city still partly controlled by another man. At the start of the new year the mayor had a respite from the troubling events of the past several months—the indictments, the urban-renewal hearings, the school fights— and began at last to feel a sense of accomplishment. In mid-January he addressed the Rotary Club with "a very exciting announcement." The courts had rejected the last appeal of the Housing Authority commissioners and every required city agency had approved the mayor's long-planned Redevelopment Authority, which held the promise of bringing development capital to Paterson. Two major middle-class housing developments, which represented the first significant dwellings to go up during his administration, were also underway. And he had mustered a delegation from the Chamber of Commerce to remind the state transportation department that the city was still being hindered by the incompleted Route 80.

At the end of the month, in a relaxed frame of mind, Kramer invited the City Hall reporters to lunch. Sitting over roast-beef sandwiches washed down by Birch beer at a small bar and grill across from City Hall, Kramer again seemed to be the enthusiastic, hopeful man who had captured his city's best instincts. The reporters were delighted to get him alone, knowing that, as the campaign progressed, there would be few random remarks from the mayor which didn't fit exactly with political calculations. Yet, as he spoke thoughtfully about his feelings for the city, the chasm between what he had thought and what he would now do became only more apparent.

Kramer considered education to be the first priority. "We have kids in our schools who don't know what a crayon is until they get in kindergarten," he noted. "Do you know what that means? The kid is beat. The only way is to teach him something so he can stand up on his own two feet." A few months later, acceding to a law-and-order campaign, Kramer would announce that the police, not the schools, were the city's budgetary priority. Despite his abrasive relations with the blacks, he still thought there was a basis for progress. "The hardest thing to do," he said, "is to find the real leadership in the black community. The guys who stand on the street corners and shout aren't the real leaders. You've got to be honest with the black community—sit down and say, 'Look, fellows, I admit this has been rape, but we can build something real.' You don't give them fake concessions to appease them. You find the constructive ones and put them on these boards where they can have some influence." The next day Kramer named three commissioners to fill vacancies on the board of education; not a black or a Puerto Rican was included.

"I don't resent criticism," the mayor maintained, "if the person doing it is doing something. What I do resent are these piranhas who circle City Hall, like the ones who call up during the riots and say, 'Shoot! Shoot!' I'd like to put the gun in their hands and see what happens." The mayor who didn't resent criticism more and more simply avoided it by conducting city business so secretly that a prominent member of his own administration remarked, "It's lucky there are newspapers in this city, or else no one would know what's going on."

A few days later Mayor Kramer completed the first month of his third (and what many regarded as his last) year in office with a finale that almost revived Paterson's long-gone days as a vaudeville center. The morning of January 29 he called an "emergency session" of the Police and Fire Board. "A visible cop is the best deterrent to crime," he announced and asked for an appropriation for fifty more policemen—raising the department's strength by one-seventh.

According to the I.A.C.P. report, the department was not undermanned; in fact, the report noted that the department's size was above average for cities of the same population. The goal of increasing the number of cops on the beat could have been accomplished more cheaply, if less dramatically, by hiring civilians to man the department's superfluity of desk jobs. In the enthusiasm for "the exciting idea of putting the old-fashioned cop back on the beat, but modernized with new equipment," no one remarked on this fact. Kramer had had enough problems with the police without forcing the men to leave their desks and actually patrol the city. The board unanimously pledged an "accelerated program."

Then the mayor who was "never going to play cops and robbers" ended the day with a trick pulled out of his predecessor's hat. He and Englehardt arranged a raid on a prostitution ring near City Hall. This well-publicized example of police work consisted of two plainclothesmen's making a date with the two girls through their pimp, paying in marked money, and waiting for Englehardt, followed by two more vice-squad detectives, to burst through the door. "The surprised trio were then informed that their 'Johns' were actually 'the law,'" the *Paterson News* explained delicately. The mayor next arrived to "witness" the arrests and declare, "This kind of operation is going to be stopped in Paterson no matter what it takes." The two dumpy Spanish girls were hauled off and the morning papers featured a picture of the mayor displaying a confiscated pistol to Englehardt. The two had little grins on their faces much like boys who have peeked into the girls' locker room.

While Kramer, who was still not certain if he would run, thus polished his image, the other candidates followed their own courses. Neil Morrison, the first black ever to run for mayor, became the first announced candidate on January 3. The campaign of the former boxer who had served time for armed robbery while a teenager was not taken seriously by the possible coalition of minorities that could put a black into office. Unfortunately Morrison, who now operated as tenant organizer, could not appear on the ballot until he received a formal pardon from the governor. Describing his campaign as "symbolic," he was really disenfranchised whereas the blacks felt they were disenfranchised in practice.

Although the governor granted Morrison's pardon, he was not in a position to put together a mayoral campaign. Tall, thin, and intense, Morrison could be spellbinding. Invited to a Candidates' Night at the Taxpayers Association, he gave that group a large dose of realism. Lowering taxes and naïve honesty, he warned, were hardly enough to save Paterson. People had to realize the depths of the city's turmoil and corruption, even that some forces were willing to foment riots to make Kramer look bad. "It was like Stalin walking into the John Birch Society," noted one observer, "and yet he gave one of the most impressive speeches I've ever heard in Paterson." At other times, however, Morrison talked distractedly about "going back to Africa" or bringing in "armed guards" to protect himself from Paterson's racists. But he did serve as a focal point for black aspirations in the city and developed a following. After dangling himself between Kramer and Graves, he finally decided that turning his forces over to Kramer held more advantages than being a symbolic candidate.

The perennial contenders jumped in. There was Dominick Angotti, who traditionally occupied the conservative line. Then came Harold Wanamaker, a genially eccentric housepainter who had made something of a hobby of running for mayor of Paterson and was making his second try as an independent. His program was straightforward.

He wanted to fill in Molly Ann Brook to provide space for urban renewal, substitute K-9 (trained attack) dogs for the police because the dogs "only need one hearty meal a day" and would save money, and return to the old system of handing out food instead of welfare to make sure kids "get the nourishment they need." Although no one took them seriously, these candidates were considered the flourishes without which no Paterson election could be complete. As a newspaper columnist wrote, "Who can say that the old girl [i.e., Paterson] is dead when ten people still want to run for mayor?" *I ever see just one buzzard flying around*

Throughout these preliminaries, however, real attention focused on the Democrats. Despite every placating syllable that Grossi could muster, the party once again had split wide open. Joseph Lazzara—owner of Lazzara's Tasty Crust Bread Company, Paterson's single largest taxpayer, possessor of an impressive home that city residents had nicknamed "The Alamo," and longtime party stalwart—decided to challenge Graves in the primary. For decades Lazzara had contributed to the party coffers and for years Grossi had promised him that the nomination for the Paterson mayoralty would one day be his. Thus far, Lazzara had risen no higher than the Board of Freeholders. He had accepted the post of being Wegner's campaign manager in 1966 on the assurance that "next time" was his. Whatever promises Grossi had made Lazzara, however, he had no choice but to whip the party into supporting Graves. It was not a task he particularly enjoyed. Like many people, the county chairman had a long-standing scorecard with the former mayor—Graves' hogging the city patronage for himself and his paltry support of the party despite his personal wealth. "Tony's heart isn't in this one," one of his cohorts noted. But no matter where Tony's heart was, he yielded to Graves.

Lazzara, in a folksy eight-page statement, offered himself as "a mayor for the '70's, the critical years ahead," and stressed his position as a son of the city. "I have a love for Paterson, the city of my birth," he declared. "Here my loving wife and I are raising five children." He also portrayed himself as an independent fighting "the Graves-Grossi combo" and bossism. Graves was not very upset by Lazzara's appearance on the scene. He saw no reason to fear a genial, graying baker whom the organization had used for years. "It's o.k. for him to run," Graves conceded. "He's a nice guy, but he can't win. The days of the nice guys are over." Nevertheless, the primary was to be the usual vicious affair that would leave many Democrats bitterly estranged from their party.

Interest focused on Kramer, who still refused to announce. Instead, Angelo ("Wahoo") Massanero, known throughout the city simply as Wahoo, became the next candidate. Wahoo, Paterson's best-loved character, had for years kept the city entertained through an astounding variety of escapades. Once, he had managed to get to Europe. When he ran out of money, the federal government was forced to ship him home. Wahoo's special talent was a constant charade on the city politic. Although he was illiterate, he felt he would make a fine mayor. "All the other bums are running. Why can't I?" was his brief, formal announcement. Later he pulled out of the race, explaining that he hadn't been able to gather enough false signatures on his nominating petition and that he felt it would be unfair for anyone to run for mayor of Paterson from an honest position.

Rooney came in formally, with backing from some of Kramer's former supporters. "The other candidates have misunderstood the problems," he stated. "The problems are taxes and welfare."

Finally, on the afternoon of March 21, Kramer summoned the press to his house, a comfortable split-level on the city's east side. He offered the reporters drinks and handed them a three-page statement without comment. Mary Ellen, who was generally thought to want her husband to withdraw, stood by. Their five-year-old daughter and two-year-old son were dressed in the matching baby-blue military outfits they wore for official occasions. The Kramers' six-month-old baby boy occupied himself by patting his sister's head as the family posed for pictures of the event. For a moment they did stand apart, apart from ambition and disappointment and the blight which had overtaken their decision to "get this city back"—taken so long ago with close friends over a cup of coffee—and they both smiled for pictures and proceeded with a campaign they dreaded.

Kramer's statement described a city which has "begun to reawaken," of a new "flavor and dedication in city government," and emphasized his contributions such as increased school aid, housing-code enforcement, Model Cities, urban renewal, and the Senior Citizens Council. "But a job begun is far from completed," it concluded. "To turn from this difficult task, trying and demanding though it has been, would be to desert our beloved city in her hour of great need. . . . My wife Mary Ellen and I have decided we must accept this awesome challenge." How different this quiet, almost bleak announcement was from 1966. Kramer now stood alone, with neither the party cohorts who had accompanied Graves nor the enthusiastic "team" who had accompanied him on his first mission.

The mayor looked distracted. Perhaps he wasn't thinking of a political campaign at all. Perhaps he was thinking of a summer evening in 1967 when he had first realized what he had done by becoming mayor of an American city. Newark had just burst into the riot that stunned a nation; Paterson lay ten miles away, tension rolling over the city like a suffocating blanket. Pat Kramer was alone in his office. His wife and aides were outside in the adjoining conference room. They had come to wait, to plan, and to pray.

For a moment the mayor looked out the window into the darkness that everyone expected momentarily to light into the flames of destruction. The street lights played over two policemen, the only human beings on the street, slowly walking by in riot helmets. Headquarters impatiently awaited an order that only the mayor could give. Was the department to shoot to kill? Paterson was too small a city for such a decision to lose its impact in the anonymity of the dead on the other side of town; the ghetto began a few blocks from City Hall, and with it, faces everyone knew. "This isn't what I ran for," the mayor thought silently, looking on the dark street. "This isn't the job I took. Please don't let this be me making this decision." But it was him; and in 1967 both he and the city escaped, but the next year, when Main Street erupted, he ordered the department to shoot armed rioters and firebombers.

Paterson now had a complete mayoral race—from its first black candidate to its incumbent.

He was finally and officially back. Graves' exile was over. He was running for mayor, and so exuberant did his return make him that he softened momentarily. For the first time, he admitted that he had made mistakes in the past. At the opening of his campaign headquarters, he deviated from his constant attacks on the Kramer administration and summoned an idealistic note. "We are joining in a cause of righteousness, a cause of decency within government, a cause of better understanding of man himself and he with me."

Graves really wanted to win this mayoralty. For the first time in his long public career, he seemed to evince a humane feeling for Paterson's aspirations and troubles. He was sincerely disturbed by the city's condition and did not think it could survive another term under Kramer. If winning Paterson meant he had to accept the city on its own terms, rather than demand that it obey him, he now seemed willing to take this approach. He adapted himself to a changed Paterson, a city that had not yet found a way to command itself, but that pulled fitfully against its reins. Graves, who had previously run his campaigns entirely by himself, taking advice from no one, now set up a special phone line on which citizens could call him day and night and "help write my platform." The *Morning Call* editorialized that all the candidates were promising law and order, but the one who added justice to this pledge would have the edge. Graves, who headlined his advertising with the slogan "The Candidate for Law and Order," became "The Candidate for Justice, Law and Order." The man who had turned a deaf ear to citizens during his own administration now became a sympathetic listener to anyone with a complaint—even against the police.

There was one area in particular where Graves had a margin. "I have that burning desire to once again give leadership to the city of Paterson," he announced. Paterson desired leadership. The city wanted competent administrators and programs such as the housing inspections that Kramer had brought in; but it was tired of "professionals" and programs' often being used to gloss over root problems. There was something extraordinarily attractive in Graves' personal, gut-level style, and he made people feel that the city belonged to them through the mayor. Playing heavily on the city's feeling of drifting in a vacuum, Graves underscored Paterson's pride in its capacity to solve its own problems—or at least to solve them through a mayor who knew how to "sit down and crack some heads together."

Yet in the midst of this renascence, glimpses of the old Graves, sounding the same, relentless theme, kept slipping through. "Could you on God's wrath want another three years of what Pat Kramer has done to this city?" he questioned. "The issue of this campaign is law and order and that's it. The first thing, January 1st, I'll order the police to start answering calls in ninety seconds again. I guarantee I'll have a police car passing every block in Paterson once every hour. And I have a feeling that we won't have to wait for January 1st because the minute the election's over, the police will start taking things into their own hands." One wag estimated that the new guarantee, that of the police passing every block every hour, would have the available number of squad cars traveling 175 m.p.h. twenty-four hours a day. But to the terrified, logistics didn't matter.

In this recharged atmosphere, Kramer faced a delicate balancing act—that of finally taking command of the police while assuring the populace that his administration would be firmly dedicated to fighting crime. In the heat of the various police scandals three months before, Kramer had announced a "coast-to-coast search for the best professional police officer in the United States." The mayor had finally discovered Paul Blubaum, the forty-four-year-old former police chief of Phoenix, Arizona. A highly competent police officer, Blubaum had won the respect of Phoenix's minority groups as well as praise from Senator Barry Goldwater, but had resigned in protest over political interference with his department. Presented to the Paterson press for an introductory session, Blubaum answered all questions honestly and briefly. He did not think the job would be easy and promised no miracles. Asked what his knowledge of the city was, he looked momentarily pained. Apparently Paterson's department was known in police circles throughout the country. "A lot of my friends advised me not to come here," he replied. "You folks have the reputation of one of the worst departments in the country."

Blubaum's arrival was exactly what Graves had been looking for—final proof that "the mayor of Boystown" was incapable of running the city. Graves invoked the city's long-standing fear of outside interference. "An outsider will absolutely destroy our department," he declared. "A sheriff from a hick town can't possibly understand Paterson. [Graves persisted in characterizing Phoenix, which was three times larger than Paterson, as a dusty wayside inhabited solely by cowpokes.] First thing you know, he'll have our police wearing cowboy hats. Phoenix doesn't even have any minorities. How could he have any idea what's going on here?" Graves immediately started a court suit to block the appointment. The well-organized opposition to the Police director mounted.

In light of the controversy created by his appointment of Blubaum and with the various sit-ins and demonstrations that had marked his administration, Mayor Kramer was hardly averse to an opportunity to give dramatic evidence of his firmness. The black students at Eastside High School conveniently provided it.

Since the trouble had first started at the high school in January, both the mayor and the board had made an art out of ignoring it. The mayor had met once with the elected student leaders and no one had met with the black students. Although the school, like most city high schools, contained a hard core of violent students, it also had student leaders of exceptional quality whom the mayor characterized as "bright, well-spoken and intelligent," as did every adult who came in contact with them.

The Black Students Organization had persistently tried to present its demands through proper channels, but the black students had made a tactical error in their demand to fly an Afro-American flag. Although it was a "symbolic" demand that they did not expect to be granted, it nevertheless provided the excuse for ignoring their serious complaints about school conditions. The mayor first came up with the theory that the B.S.O. violated New Jersey antidiscrimination laws by being only for blacks. No matter how many times the black students pointed out that they did not bar white members, the mayor persisted in characterizing it as "an illegal organization" with which the city could have no official dealings. Of all the students' demands, the one on which he commented concerned the Afro-American flag. "As long as I am mayor of this city, the American flag will never be taken down from the school. I can assure you of that." The B.S.O. had never asked to take down the American flag; they had asked permission to fly their own banner, and not on the flagpole, but inside the auditorium.

Cafeteria boycotts started at the end of February, but things quieted down in view of the board's upcoming meeting in March. Mrs. Rauschenbach first announced that the B.S.O.'s demands, once again, were not on "the official agenda" and then postponed the meeting entirely. The students who had placed their hopes in the meeting with the board felt betrayed, and their spokesmen began to change from "bright, well-spoken kids" to hostile kids. Next they proceeded to hold after-school sit-ins, which disbanded every day in the face of police action. Still no one met with them.

The school was by now in a state of chaos and a magnet for the most unstable elements in the city. Troublemakers, the curious, and some very disturbed people lined up outside Eastside each afternoon—along with television cameras from New York—hoping for the action to start. One pigtailed girl, about eleven years old, indicated the general impatience of those waiting for the signal to man the barricades. Prevented from sneaking inside to join the sit-in, she finally marched up to a startled policeman, carefully raised her leg, and kicked him in the groin. "Look, they're taking a baby!" the crowd shouted angrily as she was put in a car for the trip to the stationhouse. The last day of the sit-in arsonists set eight fires in the city. The mayor knew that these were the dangers of forcing the situation so far, but he, too, was waiting. His moment finally came on March 11, when he was inconveniently hospitalized for a pinched nerve, but nonetheless he managed his part.

That morning the students parked themselves in the auditorium and refused to leave. Mrs. Rauschenbach hastily assembled five other commissioners for a negotiating session. After several hours of discussion, the single point of disagreement was the proposal for a black vice-principal. The board had offered to create deans of men and women and appoint blacks to them, thus making the blacks not second, but third best. The students, therefore, did not accept the package, but promised they would leave the building if Dr. Gioia spoke with them. Gioia, who had been waiting for the board's results, immediately left the building himself. On the mayor's orders, cordons of police surrounded the school. Deputy Chief John Hess, a stocky man with a crew cut, gave his men a short, impassioned talk: "Keep cool. You'll be called a lot of names. Just don't get angry. And don't hit anybody. I don't want anybody taking any independent action. It may take a long time, but we'll stick to the plan." The plan was to carry out students individually.

Inside the auditorium Etta James, president of the B.S.O., gave brief but similar advice to her followers. "I don't want no stompin', no shoutin', no nothin'," she commanded.

An hour and a half later every student had been removed without incident. The policemen and civil-rights leaders left the auditorium and fell into each other's arms, relieved that there had been no violence and no injuries. But it was too soon for congratulations. The "cuckoo clocks" were still outside and a group stationed across the street began throwing bottles. For a few minutes the policemen at the school gate maintained their line and then a small, furious battle erupted.* Hess ran out of the school, astounded by the new scene. The street, which was a confusion of backed-up traffic, a growing crowd, flying bottles, and flailing nightsticks, held vicious potential. The stocky deputy chief hurriedly pulled his men behind the school gate and closed it so the two sides couldn't reach one another. His action—retreating in favor of ultimate peace—was a rare display of common sense.

Out of the hospital the next day, the mayor taped an interview with all the networks, angrily condemning the students. "Force will be met with force," he declared and said that the students wanted to throw the American flag in the garbage pail and have soul food in the cafeteria. Both charges were false.

Like many urban confrontations, the incident not only had been avoidable, but cost the city irreparable damage. It convinced children that they could gain nothing through attempts to work peacefully. As the *Paterson News* noted in an editorial blaming the entire affair on the students, the battle at Eastside had reverberated in seemingly unconnected ways. This violent image of Paterson was broadcast across the country. As a result, many businesses in the city had insurance policies canceled, developers lost interest in the city, and "a town struggling to live" incurred more problems. As for "saving the city's middle class," nothing could have more successfully encouraged whites to leave. Parents pulled their children out of Eastside as fast as they could and fled to the tranquillity of the suburbs. And in the end the board agreed to all the demands except for the flag and removing the

---

* Five policemen were later indicted on civil-rights charges as a result of this incident, but the charges were eventually dismissed.

guards—in other words, the settlement the students would have accepted from the beginning.

The following morning, the mayor sat in his office with an air of satisfaction. He had made national news. A group of factory workers from Sacramento, California, had pooled their coffee money to call him long distance and see "if Mayor Kramer really existed" to show their approval of his firm stand on the flag. Telegrams of support poured in from around the country. Two years before, if someone had told Kramer he would reach this point, he probably would have laughed; but after constant criticism from all sides, he was delighted with the coast-to-coast praise that resulted from so simple a device as protecting the Stars and Stripes from a nonexistent threat. The only discordant note came from a few black students who asked him to believe that no one had advocated throwing the flag in the garbage.

The same evening the police and the students had been left to do battle outside Eastside, the Police and Fire Board met for a public hearing on "An Ordinance Authorizing the Appointment and Employment of an Administrative Director to the Police Department of the City of Paterson"—that is to say, hiring Blubaum. The Aldermanic Chambers were packed, mainly with people who opposed the appointment. Englehardt presided as chairman while three mayoral candidates—Graves, Rooney, and Morrison—waited to give their views. Kramer had sent a message from his hospital bed asking citizens and officials alike to "rise above political partisanship" in considering the vital necessity of the appointment. Englehardt announced that, due to the extraordinary number of speakers, comments would be limited to five minutes and asked Graves if he would like to go first. "I will wait my turn," Graves responded. "I need at least a half hour."

The line of speakers took their turn at the microphone. Opinions ranged from suggesting Blubaum's salary should be donated to the indicted policemen to thinking Blubaum might bring some efficiency to the department if he wasn't given politcal interference. In the midst of the trail of speakers Corsini reached his breaking point. Like many in Paterson who had watched Graves and Kramer and found no answers, he was angry. All he saw was that the city's final protection, its "thin, blue line," was being taken away. There seemed to be no logical place to vent his feelings, so he chose the object most conveniently at hand, which happened to be Ken Hayden, clerk to the board, who was then consulting with Englehardt. "Don't you say anything! You're not a member of this board," Corsini shouted.

"Now, don't start in on me," Hayden replied.

Corsini, his cherubic face puffed in anger, reared up and punched Hayden. The two landed on the floor and Englehardt pulled the commissioner off the clerk. Corsini retrieved his snap-on tie—the only visible casualty of an encounter that clearly demonstrated the profound, aimless wrath evoked by the city's problems.

Finally Graves stepped forward and, as promised, spoke for a half hour. He accused the board of destroying the department and of bringing in a man "who has no idea of the problems of the city of Paterson." He invited the commissioners to resign since they had proven they couldn't handle their duties.

"Mayor Graves," responded Englehardt, looking very strained in this first public confrontation with the man who had launched his career, "I'll lay my cards on the table. I feel as though there's a split in the upper echelons of the department that no man in Paterson could straighten out. I couldn't do it. You can't ask a man in the department to take over, stepping on many toes, and then expect him to go back to the ranks."

"I was never aware of any friction while I was mayor,"

countered Graves. He shot his former sidekick-turned-foe a long, burning look. "All right, gentlemen. It seems to be a hopeless cause."

Blubaum officially took over his post two weeks later. Corsini's fury over the appointment did not prevent him from extending traditional courtesy to the newcomer; he invited Blubaum to be his guest for an Oldtimers' Game at Yankee Stadium.

A few days after the brawl at the school and the punch-out at the board, the sounds of "a working plant" filtered from Eastside to mingle with a bright, sunny day. Two plain-clothesmen from the Youth Guidance Division stood guard at the entrance to the old building. A teacher's voice could be heard rising shrilly from inside the building. "Now, I'm warning you people over here and you people over there." A lone piano in the basement led the melody for a music class. Young voices followed and a sweet, hopeful melody joined the first touches of spring in Paterson. They were singing "Born Free."

We must remember that every party, and every individual, is now struggling for a share in the executive and judicial power as well as legislative, for a share of the distribution of all honors, offices, rewards, and profits. Every passion and prejudice of every voter will be applied to, every flattery and menace, every trick and bribe that can be bestowed will be accepted and used.

—PRESIDENT JOHN ADAMS

The year 1969 may not have seen the best campaign Paterson had ever conducted, but it saw the most intense. The candidates themselves seemed to realize that the time for street brawls, "practical" jokes on the opposition, spirited rallies, and the other paraphernalia of campaigns past was gone. To the candidates, this campaign, in a mysterious way, was final. And they fought for the city in public and in private, in newspaper headlines and in secret arrangements, in debates and in the back tenements, with new alliances and old. Of course, Paterson would pay the bills—for Kramer's hastily conceived public works projects and Graves' sensationalistic lawsuits—and would pay, in the end, for the derangement of its government, which was part of fighting for the future.

This campaign's atmosphere was markedly different from the last. There was little talk of urban renewal, community relations, rehabilitation programs, superhighways, job training, and all the other magic phrases that had captured Paterson's attention and imagination in 1966. The issue for the city now was simple—whether to hold on and look toward a more reasonable future or to give in and go back. That Kramer had "betrayed" his original promise, as some of his early backers charged, ultimately mattered very little. He was still the hope for those who believed in the possibility of a responsive and democratic city government. That law and order under Graves had not been very orderly also did not matter. For those who saw the city being ravaged, his methods represented the only apparent defense against destruction. It was an election based not on platforms and projects, but on passionate, gut feelings.

Although the election evoked intense emotions, it was being fought for a victory that the city knew did not really exist. The turmoils of the past years had made both sides aware that there was something so profoundly wrong with the premises of life in Paterson that victory could not mean progress, change, new directions, and the other themes that victory usually signifies. Either way, after the ballots were counted, there would be no breakthrough, only the city's statement of what it aspired to become.

For a small city and considering he had started with amateurs, Kramer had an impressively sophisticated campaign operation. After working out strategy with his advisors, the mayor did not bother with details and simply appeared, smiling, at the appointments made for him. His team did everything else—canvasing, advertising, arranging speeches, and preparing a list of 3,000 registrants (five percent of the city's voters) whom they felt were open to legal challenges; they supervised the elaborate election-day machinery through highly trained poll watchers and a fleet of radio-dispatched cars to rush lawyers to trouble spots. Kramer's advertising consisted of a series of "Progress Reports," which disclosed, as the blurb put it, his "never-ending flow of bold, new ideas" in the fields of law enforcement, educaion, housing, and cultural affairs. His slogan was "Keep Kramer for Paterson's Sake," a message which opponents scribbled over to read "Keep Kramer Out for God's Sake."

In contrast to the previous campaign, gone were the street-corner rallies, walking tours, and other events promising excitement. "Before, nobody knew who I was. Obviously that's not the problem now," Kramer noted. There were, however, other reasons behind the campaign's quiet facade. Having previously won more or less on his own, Kramer did not place complete faith in enthusiastic popular support to win this election. The patient Bozzo—the man who never invested in politics or in people, the studious tactician who sat back waiting to redeal—seemed now to hold the trump card in Paterson. He might ally himself with Kramer or he might return to his old arrangements with the Democratic organization. Since Graves held so many ties to the machine, where Republican and Democrat were only different labels for common interests, Kramer had sought to protect himself from defections by moving from an uneasy to an almost open alliance with the Republican boss. These were not matters to be discussed on walking tours.

Graves was the second factor behind Kramer's understated approach. Whatever rash actions Kramer had committed in the midst of crises, he seemed to have summoned an inner calm for the campaign. He steeled himself to disregard the former mayor, refusing to answer his challenges. Above all, Kramer did not believe in the new, open, and concerned Graves; and just as Graves considered Kramer his best ammunition, Kramer considered the former mayor his best weapon. "If I let him alone long enough, he'll defeat himself. All he has to do is remind people of who he is, and he's finished." As the Kramer people went about steadily canvasing and presenting their progress reports, they desperately wanted one thing—for Graves to make his mistake.

Unlike the mayor, Graves conducted his campaign almost entirely by himself. He had a paid staff and volunteers, but their duties were minimal. Graves arranged his own schedule of appearances and wrote his own newspaper advertisements, which consisted mainly of exposés about the growth in crime and the decline in other aspects of the city's life. "Paterson cannot suffer the ineptness its educational philosophy has lost in the past three years!" declared one message. If the syntax was occasionally jumbled, Graves was nevertheless an accomplished campaigner. He enjoyed being the man who would bring government back to the people. "For the first time Paterson will truly be run on behalf of Patersonians," he promised. "I'll give you the best service you ever saw." Citizens were going to help write his platform; they could call at any hour with suggestions.

Rooney, running as an independent, had no campaign philosophy except to "tell people the truth about what's going on in Paterson." He had neither money nor a large organization since he did not believe in garnering support that way. "Who do you think pays for those $100-a-ticket dinners?" he asked. "You see people there like you and me and we don't have $100 for a dinner. Companies who want business from the city buy the tickets and we pay for it in the end." He was so stringently honest about his pledge to end all programs that, when appearing in a debate at the Senior Citizens Council, he would not even promise to keep the program that influential block of voters prized. It would be "evaluated along with everything else and only if it's really needed will we keep it." Some called him a racist; he was not, although he admitted he would accept support from Wallacites or wherever he could find it. Rooney's interpretation of "the right way" for people to behave was not universally accepted and, even had it been, Paterson, as a city, was not in a position to abide by his views. His various promises, such as refusing new welfare cases and stopping the inflow of affidavit pupils, were impossible in light of federal and state laws.

Only once in the campaign did Rooney appear to respond to a Paterson that was composed of anxious people as well as cold facts. Debating before a black audience, he suddenly cast aside his graphs, lists, slides, and appealed to his wary listeners as human beings. "I'd like to point out," he stated, "that the Taxpayers Association voted unanimously to support the firing of the two policemen in the shooting incident. We did it because they lied. The Taxpayers Association and you people are really a lot closer than you think, but the politicians want to keep you separated so they can keep everything for themselves; we just have to do things right. We don't need any more politicians using and abusing people of all colors. I want to go into the city of Paterson as responsible to responsible people."

Both Kramer and Graves considered his approach somewhat simplistic, but they also feared his appeal to conservatives and idealists alike. Graves said he was "a dreamer who would make a better congressman." Kramer called him an example of "the do-nothingism that killed Paterson." Neither, however, could really attack Rooney. Who could be against lowering taxes, stopping welfare, and promoting honesty?

Kramer started using the advantages of an incumbent to rearrange the city in his favor. First he lowered taxes. It was an artificial drop, accomplished partly by postponing the payment of city bills, which meant that taxpayers would have to make it up with interest the following year. He financed last-minute projects such as the phalanx of new foot patrolmen and a much-heralded program for replacing the city's street signs—so vandalized that it was impossible to locate streets in many sections of the city—with emergency appropriations that also would not show up until the following year.

Having handled the treasury, the mayor turned to the press. Remembering Harry B. Haines' predilection for both mothers and statues, on Mother's Day he renamed the Plaza of Memories the Harry B. Haines Plaza of Memories. At the elaborate ceremony, the mayor praised Haines for "his innumerable accomplishments on behalf of the city, none of which is more meaningful or inspirational than this lovely tribute to parents and mothers on their day." Here, too, the campaign was quite different from the days when Kramer and his aides had lambasted the *News* for its bias toward Wegner. The paper carried human-interest stories about the mayor, for instance a report about a Paterson serviceman stationed in Korea who had plastered signs along the DMZ with Kramer stickers. When Kramer had problems, the *News* noted them, but briefly.

In spite of the mayor's efforts to publicize only the positive aspects of reform, a few untidy sights were open for public view. Kramer's determination to win over the people he had once fought ended in a staggering patronage splurge. Dangling themselves between Kramer and Graves, dozens of smart operators profited. This splurge went so far that it was a little much even for the mayor's close supporters. When, for example, Kramer assented to the reappointment of "G.I. Jimmy" Vasile to a city job, City Counsel Joe Conn, also head of Citizens for Kramer, openly took issue with the mayor for the first time.

In the end, Kramer's efforts to woo the old guard threatened one of his major accomplishments. Not all changes in the police department were the mayor's doing; they came also as a result of the blacks' making clear that the police would be held accountable for their actions, and from many policemen themselves, who were sick of being used and tired of being hated. At one time, the department's reputation had been so notorious that it could not attract enough recruits to fill its regular roster. Now, in its first intensive effort to find minority members, it had managed to obtain the new patrolmen and to upgrade its performance as well. Blubaum personally interviewed all candidates. Englehardt went into Spanish neighborhoods looking for recruits and asking them "to give it a try." The department had even made some impressive hard-drug hauls. Critics charged that many of the improvements were only superficial. Nevertheless, within only a few months, the change strongly indicated that police friction is not an insoluble problem and moved the city's sometime Black Panther leader to observe that he still didn't like the old police "but these new cats, man, they're really something. They're really into it."

But the major obstacle, as Blubaum knew, rested with the "old cats." He formulated a two-stage reorganization plan designed to move one-seventh of the men from their comfortable berths at headquarters to street duty, thereby giving the city a major increase in protection at no added cost. The Police and Fire Board passed the plan unanimously, but it never really went into effect. Owing to the friction between Blubaum and the board, many policemen had managed to have their new orders rescinded. A few months later, speaking as always in his genial, understated manner, Blubaum reminded the press that he had purposely refused to sign a contract with the city and would, as promised, quit if politics interfered with departmental reform.

In the face of another crisis, Kramer was forced to call a secret session of the Police and Fire Board. It was so savage that all the participants afterward refused comment. "It would not be in the best interests of the city to reveal what went on here," Corsini noted. Apparently Blubaum had lapsed from his genial manner, particularly in discussing Englehardt's relations with the police. The director did not quit and pronounced himself "satisfied" (although he really was not) that he had the cooperation of the mayor's office, and major assignments were still made without his being informed.

In June the mayor suffered another moment of public embarrassment. At the age of seventy, Joseph G. Bozzo passed from this life. When first asked if he would like to comment publicly on Bozzo's death, Kramer replied, "Good God, no." However, he later extended his sympathy to the family and finally appeared at the funeral home. Paying final respects to Bozzo placed Kramer on a formal footing with the other mourners. Among those who came to the funeral home or attended the last rites were, for the Republicans, Carl Lembo, the housing commissioner Graves had appointed and Kramer had ousted; County Sheriff Frank Davenport; and County Counsel Jim Segreto. Mrs. Betty Van Dine Smith, the Supervisor of Elections, wept quietly. Joseph Muccio cried openly. The Democrats did not forget their sometime friend, sometime opponent. Tony Grossi and Ralph Gamotese, Graves' former private secretary, appeared. From Hudson County came John V. Kenney, "Boss" Hague's heir, and a man soon to be jailed as the price for becoming a legend in his own time. It could only be at a funeral where the people of Passaic County would receive an open view of the forces controlling their lives.

These may not have been inspiring company for a reform mayor, yet Kramer attended. Although Joseph G. Bozzo

had died, his legacy remained—in the tenements bled by
corruption, in the windowless courthouse, in the fear and
apathy that pervaded the city, and most specifically in
Kramer's chances for reelection. Mrs. Smith still controlled
the Board of Elections; all the anxious ward leaders, county
hacks, and other functionaries, now without a chief, might
decide that their safest path lay in making up with the
Democrats. And there was still that momentous day in the
future when public sentiment would count for little and the
real issue would be how many legal voters could actually
claim their right to pull the lever.

Frank X. Graves had not yet made a mistake; he was
still shaking hands with everyone, promising the "best service
you ever saw," and running almost daily ads on the city's
crime statistics. In August he scored a coup. The state
legislature passed the first urban-aid package in New Jersey's
history, allocating $12 million to be shared among the six
largest cities. The final allocation was based on a complex
formula, including the individual cities' crime and tax rates.
Paterson, originally figured to receive $1.4 million, got only
$900,000. Taxes were down, and so apparently was crime.
When Kramer learned of the allocation formula, he desperately tried to retrieve the lost funds, firing off telegrams
accusing the state of "penalizing the city for progress."

Graves, however, charged that the city lost the money
because crime figures had been reported erroneously during
the Kramer administration. He had obtained the police department's stolen-car log book, which technically was classi-
fied information. The department had only reported half
the number of stolen cars to the state attorney general's
office. Graves said he thought other crime categories were
erroneous, but he had no proof. (After extensive study, the
Morning Call concluded the reporting of crime figures had
not been much different during either administration, leav-

ing a large question of accuracy in both cases and putting the loss at $200,000.)

A few weeks later Kramer nudged Graves into making his mistake. In a special ceremony, Sergeant Peter Le Conte was named the city's "top cop," a newly created honor, and was given a special citation for having received more medals and awards than any other policeman. Following this, number four in a series of "Progress Reports" appeared and the city almost let out an audible gasp. Large newspaper ads featured Le Conte, formerly Graves' fair-haired boy and a command officer in the élite Tactical Patrol Force Graves had started. The twenty-eight-year veteran of the Paterson Police Department gazed sincerely from the page, his battered face sporting a benign smile. He explained Kramer's "new concept" in police work, the community-affairs program which prevented crime before it occurred and turned the police into friends. When asked how this startling conversion had occurred, Kramer only smiled. "I think it's wonderful, a tough sergeant like that, and now he's talking about civil rights all the time. He's a dramatic example of the kind of change we've been trying to make in the department." "A man with an indictment hanging over his head will do anything," observed one skeptic of Le Conte's new role.

Graves was furious. Not only was Le Conte a hero to the law-and-order stalwarts, but Graves had never experienced such a personal betrayal. Graves, however, reserved his wrath for another, the person who had once been his close friend and who had gained power through his association with the former mayor. Englehardt's double-dealings wrenched Graves to the point that he lost his famed political sense in an all-out effort to discredit his bowling-alley partner. Graves made speeches and ran extensive advertising against the police commissioner charging that the department was "politically corrupt."

This tactic proved to be an error. Many Patersonians

had not grasped the discrepancy between Englehardt's private dealings and his public insistence on absolute law enforcement. Even Englehardt's critics could not derive much satisfaction in an attack from the very man who had launched the police commissioner's career. But once Graves had started in this vein, he did not stop. In the face of so many desertions—Le Conte, Haines, Englehardt, Vasile—he behaved like a martyr taking on the task of saving the city alone. He denounced his old comrades, railed against anything connected with the Kramer administration, and assailed the newspapers for "a conspiracy" to give him bad coverage—a conspiracy that was somewhat hard to imagine in view of the intense competition between the two papers. For the public, it was difficult to follow these contradictions and accusations.

Although Kramer felt that Graves had indeed made his mistake, he nevertheless continued to move carefully. There were still too many secret threats, secret promises, and factors beyond his control. In September, for example, some typical Graves tactics surfaced. Women were calling homes in working-class areas pretending to take a survey on busing for the board of education. Unsigned letters were sent to a residential area claiming that the Kramer administration was about to approve the construction of a rooming house nearby—with all its visions of transients, addicts, and rapists. There was also no way the mayor could be certain that his friends were still his friends. The Small Businessman's Mutual Aid Association, in conjunction with the League of Women Voters, asked the county Board of Elections to open additional registration sites in the ghetto. Mrs. Smith refused even after the League threatened legal action. She said registration facilities were "already adequate." (A study released by Rutgers University ten days earlier had shown that one half of the city's eligible voters were not registered.) The S.B.M.A.A. and the League had only wished to rectify the minorities' lack of influence in the democratic process.

Nevertheless, in the poorer sections of the city Kramer would find more support than would Graves.

Monday, November 3, was the day when Paterson's political organizations finally prepared for the process that outweighs all the plans, speeches, expenditures, and dinners which officially make up an eight-month campaign. In one moment all could be wiped out if the polls weren't fiercely guarded. For the first time Graves knew he could not control the polling places through official channels, i.e., the police and the prosecutor's office; Kramer had assigned the new walking patrolmen to election day duty. But the former mayor could still depend upon poll watchers from the Democratic organization. Kramer did not possess this luxury and had to be prepared to deal with both the Republican and Democratic organizations. His own volunteers had received a seminar in election law and he had insisted that poll watchers from the Republican organization take it also. "They weren't too enthusiastic," he noted. "They said, 'What do you mean? I've been watching polls for thirty years.' Yeah, well I know how they've been watching polls for thirty years."

That evening Graves began a series of eight dinner meetings with his workers that kept him going until past midnight. The first one, at the Redwood Tavern in the Totowa section, was an exclusively white gathering of some thirty-five men and women. Graves appeared to be relaxed and confident, addressing the group with none of his usual heated accusations. Instead, he created a quietly evangelical sense that the people of Paterson had been wronged, by Kramer's misdeeds, by unfair newspapers, by betrayers such as Le Conte and Englehardt. "This is more than just a Democratic worker going to the polls," he stated. "This is a Patersonian trying to free himself from the stagnation that has taken place. Guard and guard carefully tomorrow. Fight like you were the candidate yourself, because, as I have told you on many occasions, you *are* the candidate. When I'm your mayor, you'll be proud to say, 'I'm from Paterson, come up and see me some time,' " he concluded to enthusiastic applause.

It was a masterly speech, in which Graves played on the associations closest to his audience's heart, their feelings for family and for Paterson as a home; and, above all, he played upon their profound sense of having somehow been robbed —by the government, by the politicians, by a hundred other forces—of the values they knew and believed in. It was not a show. After three years of yearning for the only public office he had ever wanted, Graves seemed to hope, with victory so near, that these values could, after all, become the decisive issues.

Meanwhile, Kramer met with workers at his Market Street headquarters, gave them a brief pep talk, and went home. He was mayor of a city where honesty was at least out front; a city where a resident had a chance to complain against a landlord and where the police no longer beat up people in broad daylight; a city with some prospect of re-building. But it was still a city where many things were better left unsaid.

Downtown Paterson was finally dark. Main Street was silent and deserted. The lamps overhead lent an eerie cast to shoddy wares piled in the windows of discount stores: John's Bargain Store; ANY SHOE for $3.33; the 5 & 10. Bathed in neon on a motionless street, the displays of dish-towels, the plastic shoes, and the acetate dresses seemed as if they might disintegrate before any shoppers came to claim them. Suddenly the Rooney motorcade appeared, on its way home from the last rally. Rooney rode ahead in the sound truck, which played a military jingle. The motorcade quickly passed by, disappearing over the bridge that crossed the Passaic near the site of the former Godwin Tavern, where Washington had slept during the Revolution.

The wake of the motorcade left a terrible vision: the half-light of the street lamps which captured no movement or activity, the windows crammed with imitation goods, the far-off sound truck providing a ghostly echo of human ambition in a deserted street where there was no one left to listen. What was to become of this Main Street? Was silence the answer to Hamilton's ingenuity and Roswell Colt's greed and immigrant hope and assassins' hate and poets' dreams? Was darkness to be the last visitor to this Main Street, this Main Street which had seen the shadows of Washington, Lafayette, Grant, Eisenhower, Kennedy, and King?

Tuesday dawned with the peculiar, startling beauty of autumn sunlight. The city was electric: at corners, in coffee shops people talked with enthusiastic mutual interest. Despite diametric views of what the outcome should be, the election brought the city a sense of community that seemed to transform it. It was clear from the start, however, that November 4 was going to be a rough day.

The third district of the Seventh Ward is one of those pockets of Paterson which seems no longer to be attached to time or life. Its red-brick factories, once the bulwark of the city's power, lie abandoned like industrial brontosauri, with vines and weeds licking at their remains. Its residential pattern bears no relation to urban planning, neighborhood development projects, or Model Cities, but is, instead, a matter of which tenements have or have not burned or fallen down. The third district is touched only by two profferings of government: welfare for those who understand the rules, and jail for those who don't. Primarily blacks and Puerto Ricans occupy the third district. A number of elderly whites, barely surviving on Social Security, fill their days begging leftover food from the few small groceries. In conjunction with a series on the Task Force, the *Morning Call* interviewed some of the elderly in this area and asked them why

they didn't seek assistance; but they had heard of neither the
Task Force nor the city's own Senior Citizens Council. The
third district was even devoid of the last-minute election
improvements. The new street signs had not yet made their
way there and the polling place itself was a deserted storefront. The American flag in the window was so old it showed
only forty-eight stars.

Mrs. Anna Palma, the district co-leader, was a local
legend. Officially the fiftyish woman worked as an "investigator" in the prosecutor's office, and before each election she
visited every registrant in the third district. For a decade
she had turned in larger Democratic pluralities than those
from any other districts in the city. Election day was Mrs.
Palma's big day and she dressed carefully for the occasion,
wearing a white knit coat and her "fancy" glasses with white,
hexagon-shaped lenses. Mrs. Palma stood outside the storefront, guarding the machines inside from intruders. A Puerto
Rican of about thirty approached, wearing a Republican
button on his jacket. Mrs. Palma immediately challenged his
place of residence. "He don't live there; his sister lives there.
I'll have him arrested right now. She's on welfare; she's got
two kids. I'll have her investigated tomorrow morning."
Mrs. Palma spoke loudly so the other waiting voters were
certain to understand the situation; technically a woman
on welfare was not allowed to have her brother spend the
night.

The Republicans had specially assigned Sheriff Frank
Davenport and County Counsel Jim Segreto to deal with
Mrs. Palma. A burly man, whom people jokingly said was
so heavy "because he'd like to fit in Joe Bozzo's shoes,"
Segreto withered after the first assault. "Don't intimidate the
voters that way, Anne. You can't arrest him," was all he said.

Sheriff Davenport, a white-haired gentleman known
for his air of avuncular kindness, chimed in. "He can sign

the affidavit. That's the law. Then, if he's wrong, he can be arrested afterward."

Recitation of the law only exasperated Mrs. Palma. "Don't you tell me," she rejoined. "I don't go for that. I've got thirty-five years' experience. Call Grossi," she directed an aide. "Get him over here right away."

The Republicans summoned City Counsel Conn as their back-up man. According to the law, a committee of two Democrats and two Republicans was supposed to decide, in cases of a challenge, if a voter could go ahead. When the committee tied, the voter could proceed after signing an affidavit that made him liable to legal penalties if he lied. Since one member of third district's committee was then out to lunch, the man was advised to reappear in half an hour. Mrs. Palma started to leave in her dusty black Galaxie; as her car turned the corner, she turned back and shouted, "I'll make an example of that one right now."

A young Puerto Rican woman stood watching the fracas. Election day was her big day, too. She was helping the Democrats, which for one day out of the year gave her a glimpse of the powers that ruled her world. She also was wearing her finery—a fake leopard coat with one button left. "He couldn't live there," she remarked to no one in particular. "My people are like a circus. You know, just like a circus. They are always moving and putting on another show, opening up their tents some place else. Maybe he lived there before, but he don't live there now. Anyway, I tell him, don't do it. The big shots say they are going to help you now. But wait and see. Later you'll be left with the trouble and no big shots will come to help you."

To general surprise, the silent Puerto Rican did return in a half hour. He made no comment and only covered his face with an apologetic smile every time someone yelled at him. At one point ten law-enforcement officers, including assistant county prosecutors, policemen, the county counsel, and the sheriff, stood in front of the worn flag arguing whether or not this silently persistent man should obtain his rights. They seemed to care little about the waiting citizen. Democrat or Republican, they all worked in the windowless courthouse and what really counted was keeping their jobs, positions, and privileges. The immediate question was decided when a young Puerto Rican boxer, working for Kramer, placed *patria* above politics and quietly advised the man that voting wasn't worth the trouble to himself or his sister. This scene was repeated hundreds of times on election day in Paterson.

The polls closed at 8:00 P.M. Returns in Paterson are not subject to any modern form of computerization, so they came in quickly. Workers from each district called, drove, or simply ran to their headquarters with the news. It was clear by 8:30 that Kramer had won. At Graves' headquarters the mood was ugly. The former mayor had called his supporters and advised them to go home, but no one knew where to locate him. Kramer started the two-block walk from his headquarters to the Alexander Hamilton Hotel. He was greeted with delirium, kissed by women, and mobbed. The pressing crowd pushed him into the hotel's dining room, where his wife, Mary Ellen, stood by with a dazed smile.

The mayor started to speak. "What possible words can a candidate employ at such a time?" he asked. "You applaud Mary Ellen and me, but we should applaud you." The polite applause that followed indicated that the nearly hysterical audience did not want to applaud themselves; they wanted to celebrate their release from the past, from fear, from chains real and imagined. "You have proved that the old machinery that ground out elections is dead forever!" Kramer exclaimed. That was what the people wanted to hear, and the festivities began. Paterson's own Joe Pizza sang "The Impossible Dream." It happened to be Rooney's official campaign song; but the city itself might someday win the right to the title. Rooney himself later arrived and gave a gracious statement. "Well," said the mayor, "Harold Wanamaker's conceded, Tom Rooney's conceded, but I still haven't heard from Frank Graves. And I expected to hear from him in ninety seconds." Everyone laughed, and laughed a bit harder perhaps to make up for the fact that Frank Graves had evaded them again.

The man who had courted his city so many times and won her did not hear Paterson that night. He did not stay in a place that had deserted him. Yet in a strange sense he and the city were still part of each other; Paterson did not know final defeat and neither did he. He would never issue a concession statement. He had climbed into the Oldsmobile 88 that he called "my machine" and was speeding aimlessly down the Garden State Parkway with headlights from the darkness flashing over his own waves of exhaustion.

After that one brief day of joy, Paterson returned to normal life. On Wednesday, November 5, the state transportation department announced that it was again postponing bids on the still uncompleted Route 80. In County Court, Judge Edward Johnson sentenced Ronald Fiorilla, one of the policemen involved in the burglary ring, to a $500 fine on a charge of misconduct in office. Louise Taylor, forty-one, recently released from Graystone State Mental Hospital, was sitting quietly in Glazer's Bar when she unexpectedly reached into her purse, pulled out a gun, and fired five shots into the bar. Ella Paine of River Street spent the day fishing; she returned home to find her television set stolen. Eustachio D'Errico, eighty, of the Riverside section, died at St. Joseph's Hospital; the retired laborer had come to the United States in 1913 and left four sons, five daughters, sixteen grandchildren, and two great-grandchildren. It was indeed a normal day for Paterson or any other city—an unwelcome announcement from the state, the death of an immigrant who had arrived the year of labor's great fight against the industrial machine and died during the intense fight of citizens against the political machine, a policeman standing in court as a defendant, and a moment of madness in a bar.

A short time after the joy had settled into analysis, Kramer paused to reflect. "They were so nasty to us," he recalled. "I didn't say much about it during the campaign because it would have looked like sour grapes, but I hadn't taken my hand off the Bible the first time around when they began attacking us. That prosecutor's office is full of political appointees and they're supposed to be making a fair election? And, you know, that's what defeated them in the end." Kramer had hoped to win by 2,000 votes. He had won by 5,000. "The extra 3,000 weren't for me," he noted modestly and probably correctly. "They were the people who had been strong-armed and lied to and who were fed up." Did he regret anything? "I guess the only thing I would censure myself on was Eastside," he said long afterward. "I knew that a lot of what the kids were asking was fair and that it made sense educationally. But all I remarked on was the flag. I played it like a politician to get my credibility back; however, we did give them what they wanted in the end."

Frank X. Graves pretty much retired from the public eye. He gave an interview to the *Morning Call* in which he said he had enjoyed this campaign more than any other, that for the first time in his life he had gotten close to people and "shared my thoughts with them." Perhaps it was true that "a man in himself is a city" and that Frank Graves, along with Paterson, was groping toward some sense of community. Graves also vowed he would never again run for public office in Paterson.

And so the Paterson election was consigned to the books—briefly noted as the ordinary return of an incumbent or an example of shifting alliances in the cities or proof of the new influence of the Republican party. But the visitor who has spent so much time here knows that Paterson goes beyond such facile analyses. Paterson had every reason to seek an easy way out; but the city did not choose to do so. Underneath its hates and fears and confusions, the city's fiber ran strong. That Paterson's leaders did not deserve this faith was another matter. That Kramer, who had made it possible, had also in some respects broken his trust, was another of the city's bitter ironies. How much of it had been necessary —the alliance with Bozzo, the debacle at Eastside? But those were questions for another day.

What is important is what Paterson asked. The city had been home to so many dreams—Hamilton's industrial empire, L'Enfant's most elegant city, Patch's drunken glory, Haywood's socialist revolution—and all it had asked was a chance to be itself. It may be that Paterson has gone as far as it can go alone. The city cannot halt the flow of drugs to its own citizens while national agencies pursue haphazard law-enforcement efforts. It cannot pay for the education of its children under a disproportionate tax system. It cannot build homes without mortgages. Even after cleaning up its own government to some extent, it cannot function normally in an urban structure in which it is abused by every other level of government.

"Paterson _is_ history," Frank X. Graves once observed. And its history—the neglect, the powerlessness, the corruption, the injustice toward its residents as people and itself as a city—is the history of urbanization in the United States. It would be futile to pretend that this heritage of anomaly, violence, and alienation can be erased. Allowing Paterson real control over its own workings will not solve everything. On the other hand, the urban condition is not accidental; it is the result of the most persistent and blatant failure of American life. Like all cities, Paterson deserves finally to obtain its rights; the courage its people showed, trying again in the face of overwhelming odds, is a quality too vital to cast aside.